MW01227713

Sell while you Sleep

Turn your knowledge into an automated online business and create a life of freedom

By

KRISSY CHIN

Sell While You Sleep: Turn your knowledge into an automated online business and create a life of freedom

Copyright 2024 Krissy Chin
All rights reserved. No portion of this book may be reproduced in any form, by any means, electronic or mechanical, including photocopying, recording, or by any information storage and retrieval system, without permission in writing from the publisher.

987654321
First Edition
Printed in the United States of America.

Cover design and interior images by Claire VanBemmelen, GROworkspace
Interior layout by Jan Zucker, Pithy Wordsmithery
Copy Editing by Nils Kuehn, Pithy Wordsmithery
Proofreading by Scott Marrow, Pithy Wordsmithery

ISBN:979-8-9896653-0-3 (paperback)
ISBN: 979-8-9896653-2-7 (ebook)
ISBN: 979-8-9896653-1-0 (hardcover)

Krissy Chin
support@kandccreative.com
www.kandccreative.com

Library of Congress Control Number: 2023922967

PRAISE FOR *SELL WHILE YOU SLEEP*

"Making money while you sleep, or go on vacation, or sit at your kids' soccer game, is not only possible; it's easier today than ever! In *Sell While You Sleep*, my friend Krissy Chin gives you the playbook to build a business that not only makes you money but more importantly gives you back your time."

—Graham Cochrane,
TEDx speaker and author of
How to Get Paid for What You Know

"Everyone talks about making money in their sleep, but no one explains how to do it—except for Krissy Chin. This is the book I wish I had when I started my business; it would've saved me hundreds of mistakes and thousands of dollars. She shares an in-depth, no-fluff guide with everything you need to know, from turning your skills into offers to making sales while you sleep!"

—Mya Nichol,
Instagram expert and business coach

"Krissy will lovingly push you from questioning the impossible to seeing what's possible in all areas of your life and business. Whether you're a curious newbie or a seasoned entrepreneur, Krissy's expertise provides the missing pieces you need to build a thriving online business."

—Sage Polaris,
copywriter to the stars and conscious-launch strategist

"*Sell While You Sleep* is a supply of knowledge for anyone looking to run a successful online business. Though selling is a top priority for any business, managing money effectively is what ultimately generates profit. Krissy Chin navigates readers through both these aspects well, providing valuable insights and tips on how to make the most out of their sales and manage finances effectively. Chin's book is a valuable guide for anyone seeking to build a profitable and sustainable business."

—Melissa Houston,
author of *Cash Confident*

"As a lifelong advocate for achieving balance in our hectic lives, I'm thrilled to recommend *Sell While You Sleep*. This insightful book is much more than a guide to financial success; it's a journey towards reclaiming your time for what truly enriches your life. The strategies outlined here are practical yet transformative, offering a path to not just wealth but genuine contentment in both your personal and professional life. It's a heartfelt reminder that pursuing our dreams is not just possible but essential for our fulfillment. *Sell While You Sleep* isn't just a book; it's a beacon of hope and inspiration."

—Dave Braun,
3x international best-selling author of the
Oola: Find Balance in an Unbalanced World book series

"Krissy Chin will inspire you, light your pants on fire, and give you the practical steps to actually make your business a success. She gets real with you and also reminds you to be gentle with yourself on the way to your dreams. She opens the curtain and shows both the huge successes and the tough stuff that comes along with business. Follow her guidance in *Sell While You Sleep* and you're certain to build the business (and life) of your wildest freaking dreams."

—Ciara Rubin,
author of *You Always Know: 4-Step Guide for Empaths to Stop Second Guessing & Trust Your Intuition*

"What most people call problems or roadblocks to building a business Krissy Chin only sees as solutions and systems! Out of her experience in working with so many in business, Krissy has been able to figure out how to automate success. In *Sell While You Sleep*, you'll learn everything from tips on mindset to digital solutions to turning your hopes and dreams into hardcore, attainable goals. Highly recommend to all entrepreneurs!"

—Dr. Jim Bob Haggerton,
@DoctorJimbob, redeemedhealth.com

"Krissy Chin has masterfully written the ultimate guide on how to create a thriving business, with the freedom and dream family life you desire. If you want to unleash the magic within you, study and practice all the principles in *Sell While You Sleep*!"

—John Roussot,
award-winning business coach,
leadership trainer, and entrepreneur, and
author of best-selling book *Liberate Your Greatness*

DEDICATION

To my father, Robert VanBemmelen, who passed away before he could take his patented double dog leash to market. Thank you for always sharing your bizarre, yet practical, ideas and inventions with us and passing down those magical genes that give me a million new ideas every day.

To my children, for being my inspiration to keep working hard to follow my dreams. May you grow up to follow your own dreams and be a light to this world through your natural gifts and talents.

Download the workbook and additional resources that accompany this book at kandccreative.com/bookresources

or scan the QR code.

FOREWORD

If you have a fire in your belly and are flowing with ideas about how to build your own business and empire—but are also battling fears of, "How in the world do I get started!?"—working with Krissy Chin and her team will help you take those fearful first steps into entrepreneurship more confidently and shape your business plan, objective, and website.

Krissy and her team make you ask yourself such hard and thoughtful questions as, *What do I want? Whom do I want to serve? How can I enjoy life more?*

Krissy, her team, and the programs they've created are an absolute gift—one that is profoundly necessary in a world where you want your brand, messaging, and offerings to stand out in the market. Through our work together, I became clear on my vision, my offerings, and the language I wanted to use with my clients and was able to confidently launch my high-performance coaching and keynote-speaking business.

As a result, in less than one year, I have been able to launch digital and in-person offerings, use my website to stand out, and retire from my more-than-21-year corporate career. Krissy, thank you for being an inspirational role model who exudes working smart on your passions while balancing the joys of motherhood.

—Megan Kuiper,
CEO of MK Life on Purpose, creator of Time to Shine self-paced workshop, and keynote speaker
<u>megan-kuiper.com</u>

TABLE OF CONTENTS

IMPORTANT!
READ THIS FIRST!

Dear friend,

What if I told you that you could have a thriving business that makes $60,000 a month while working less than 20 hours a week? Well, I did it—and so can you.

Society teaches us to stay in line, be quiet, follow the rules, do as we're told, keep our heads down, and work our 9 to 5. What if, though, the fear of breaking from this "conditioning" is the very thing that's holding you back from unleashing the magic within you? What if you could make the world shine brighter and create your dream life through that magic?

What if stepping out of line allows you to walk a different path that unlocks your true purpose in this life? What if sharing your voice will make a difference? What if speaking up allows not just your voice to be heard but also your message to be delivered, providing space for lives to be changed around the globe? What if breaking the rules and doing things differently allows you to tap into something bigger, something deeper, something that requires taking a chance?

What if doing the opposite of what you have been told unlocks your full potential to create a life so blissful that people think you're faking how good it truly is?

Maybe this all sounds like a dream—but it shouldn't. For many of us, we're the only ones standing in our way. That's because so many of us actually have a deep-rooted fear of failing and not being successful. You may think you aren't smart enough or that you don't look the part. Maybe you think you aren't well spoken, or you get nervous on camera, or you're not techie enough.

What if I told you the only difference between the two of us is that I figured out how to push through my fear of publicly falling flat on my face?

I'm not saying it was always easy or that I didn't have the same fears you may be having right now. Your fears are understandable and biologically driven. As humans, we are driven by an innate survival instinct, so it's natural to freeze when you think about trying something new—like launching that new course or leaving the corporate job you worked so hard to get. And to do what? To follow your heart and step out on your own? Your brain says, "Wait a minute; that doesn't seem so safe. What if I don't make money? What if no one buys what I'm selling? What if I ruin my reputation? What if I make a fool of myself?"

I get it, but consider this:

- What if Steve Jobs had let those same fears take over?

- What if Elon Musk hadn't followed through on his big dreams?

- What if Sara Blakely had given up on her dream of making comfortable women's shapeware?

- What if Madam C.J. Walker had been too scared to sell her home-care hair products?

- What if Oprah had just stayed content being a local news anchor?

I'm sure you would agree that the world would be a much different place.

The world needs you to take a chance on yourself and be your own cheerleader first. It needs you to acknowledge the fear, thank it for being there, and then let it know that it is no longer needed. The world needs you to take action, to feel dumb the first time, to make mistakes, but to then grow. The cost of your inaction is an injustice to the world and to yourself; not only are you withholding your blessings and gifts, but you are not in a position to receive the abundance of joy and prosperity that are your birthrights.

No matter where you are in your journey to create and launch your business, there will always be moments when you question what you are doing and are afraid to take the next step. But it is imperative that you push through like a team of Navy SEALs bound and determined to complete their mission. Those are the defining moments. Those are what separate the dreams from the new realities.

Ten years ago, I dreamed of living a more purpose-driven life that would still allow me to stay home with my kids. I pictured a bank account so full that I could buy a plane ticket any time

I wanted or rack up a $1,000 clothing bill and not even flinch. While trying to figure out how to live that dream, I just kept putting one foot in front of the other as my dad had always taught my sisters and me to do. Keep moving forward. Do the next thing, take a chance, and learn.

Exactly one year after launching my first failed course, my partner and I introduced a new brand that generated our first $100,000—in just *four* months! Though one year can feel like an eternity, it can also feel like a flash of light, coming and going as quickly as a shooting star in the sky.

If you are afraid to pivot in your career, to put yourself out there on the internet, to launch your first digital offer, to hire that coach, to splurge on a new website, remember that *we are a species of evolution and growth, and in order to achieve that growth, we need to take chances and accept change—because change is the catalyst for growth.*

Visualize the moment when you stepped into your first job as an adult. Maybe you had gone to school and studied to be in a different role but took a chance and embraced change by accepting the job. I bet it taught you things you hadn't known before and helped you grow and develop in ways you couldn't have predicted. Sometimes we have to do scary things to get where we want to go.

Just imagine the risks and chances that were taken to evolve from horses and buggies to automobiles to commercial flights to space travel. These innovations would never have happened were it not for scared humans taking chances.

You were designed to change. And as you grow, you will also *outgrow.* Things that felt aligned before will now be out of alignment with where you want to go. You'll be like a snake that, in order to grow, needs to shed its old skin. If you want the time and financial freedom you dream of, you need to release what is no longer serving you so you can step into your greatness and launch your offer to the world.

If you hold onto your old skin because of fear, how do you think you will feel in a year's time? Radiating with joy and excitement or tied down with anger and resentment?

But what if you released that fear? How could your life change? Saying that nothing major can happen in a year is like forgetting the fact that human life can be created in just 10 months! If you can birth a baby within that time, you can certainly birth a business!

When my business partner and I launched our second business with an automated sales funnel, we grew from $100,000 in revenue to $1 million in just over a year. You read that correctly: **one hundred thousand to one million dollars in just over one year.**

A lot can happen in one year. And it can happen for you too!

The magical part is this: you have NO idea what 365 days from now will look like until you get there. If someone had told me while I was in nursing school, "You're going to work a few years, quit, launch a couple businesses, and then become a successful business coach," I would have said, "WHAT? That sounds crazy! I know nothing about business!"

But what I did know about was following my dreams. I believed things were possible even when I didn't know "how." I knew to keep putting one foot in front of the other, asking the experts questions, listening for the answers, turning inward, playing, exploring, and following my heart. I took chances and pivoted from where I originally thought I was going.

My partner and I shed our old skin, allowing us to help others turn their knowledge and passions into digital offers so they too could have the life they dream about. The same magic is available to you if you follow the signs, listen to your intuition, and go for it. Anyone can achieve the unimaginable! You could be in a totally different place in three months, let alone one year or five years, with a thriving business working part-time hours. And by reading this book, you're taking the big first step. Congratulations!

With time, there is no choice but to move forward, so make it your mission to move and flow with it. Keep taking action no matter how messy—even if you aren't sure where you are going because the only way to step through the right door is to put one foot in front of the other. And I promise you, if you keep moving forward, follow the steps laid out here in this book, and act, you will step into the right room. It's not a matter of if; it's a matter of when.

If you are the kind of person who is striving for a better life, then it's imperative you take that leap of faith and leave the past behind so you can create space for something new. If you desire a life of time and financial freedom, here's your full permission to step out of line, to talk when you've been told to be quiet, to break the rules, and to try something new— like launching your first digital offer—because without brave souls like you taking chances and sharing your gifts with the world, the world can't possibly turn into a better place. Use this book to help save time and avoid missteps. Let it teach you how to take your passion and turn it into a profitable business so you can start living the life of your dreams.

xo Krissy

PRO TIP

Listen and read at the same time to increase comprehension.

No, this isn't just a marketing shtick to sell more books. Listening to the audio book while reading the physical or e-book at the same time—called "immersion reading"—engages multiple parts of the brain, enhancing overall comprehension. If you are anything like me and struggle to stay focused and understand what you are reading, you may find a lot of value in this strategy. Give it a try and see how you like it!

PART I

CREATING AND SELLING YOUR OFFER

CHAPTER 1

DEFINE YOUR DREAM LIFE

Jealousy overtook me as I drove past Lake Michigan on the way to the University of Chicago Hospital, the sun glowing overhead in the summer sky. Lake Shore Drive's walking/biking paths were busy with active people. The parks were filled with blankets, families grilling burgers and playing games, and friends playing volleyball on the beach in the distance. The pit in my stomach would not go away sitting in that driver's seat in my scrubs, a 12-hour nursing shift in front of me.

I knew my life needed to change. Why hadn't anyone talked to me about "lifestyle" before I'd spent four years and six figures on a nursing degree? If someone had told me that, as a hospital nurse, I would get stuck with nights, weekends, and holidays, I might have chosen something else.

I had incredible FOMO (fear of missing out) on time I would never get back with friends and family sharing epic, memory-making, this-will-never-happen-again kind of fun. I continuously felt like I was missing out on all the super-cool stuff everyone was doing while I was working. My imagination went wild. I imagined everyone at the BBQ having the time of their lives. Maybe that was happening and maybe it wasn't, but what *was* real were my feelings. I wanted something different, and I started to dream about the future life and self I wanted.

This is my challenge to you. Dream about the life you want to live and work to make that happen. This is the fun part! Let's describe your financial and work-life goals and consider your readiness to take risks, your ability to set boundaries, and the attitude that will help you get where you want to go.

Finances

Describe in detail the financial life you would like to have. I'll share my dream finances first; then you can give it a try. In my dream life, I don't have to look at my bank account to make ordinary purchases or even to make *extraordinary* purchases. I could be strolling in an upscale mall, filled with the smell of leather—and money. I could be purchasing designer bags, sunglasses, and shoes before I stop for lunch with a friend. I could spend thousands of dollars without worrying.

This dream extends beyond shopping without a budget. My husband and I would have investments that make us money so that we have little day-to-day work. We would be able to give more back to the community in ways in which we are passionate: creating jobs and donating to charities such as Hope for Justice, which works to end human trafficking, rescue its victims, and restore their lives.

We would have a sprawling property with a well-manicured landscape and a home big enough for large family get-togethers.

We could afford daily housekeeping. A second home would be on a peaceful cove with a wake boat and plenty of water toys to keep the guests busy all day. Our double-decker dock provides a place to gather with friends where the kids run around us, yelling "cannonball!" as they fly off the top deck and land in the water and we watch the sky turn from blue to purple to red and orange with the passing of the evening hours.

I envision a third home on the beach that comfortably accommodates 20 of our friends, family, and retreat guests at any one time with the salty air wafting in through the open windows—the sound of the seagulls our continuous background music. We outsource the burden of management and upkeep of the home to a company that is well suited for the task. Not only do we have access to our beach home at a moment's notice, but it is also an investment, an appreciating asset that continues to build wealth.

We travel whenever we want. Every few months, we visit our family in Michigan. In the spring, we vacation to warm destinations; in the fall, we travel where the trees are bold and beautiful with splashes of reds and oranges set against a crisp blue sky. Our kids learn to ski during our long weekend trips to the mountains in the winter. Once a year, we travel internationally to immerse ourselves in new cultures and experience invigorating adventures.

With the comfort that comes with secure financials, I wake up every day optimistic for the day to come and with gratitude for everything around me. I look forward to the smallest memories and the largest experiences—all held in each day's potential.

Now it's your turn to imagine your dream life and all its details. Describe what your dream financial life feels, looks, smells, tastes, and sounds like.

Work Life

As you create your dream work-life scenario, instead of describing what a typical day would look like, because no one day should be "typical," focus on what the ebb and flow of a week or month would include. Let's start by looking at the week.

For me, that means I am completely checked out from work Friday through Sunday. On Fridays, I love the free time I have to spend on activities that recharge and fill me up—getting a massage, grabbing lunch with a friend or my sister, running errands I have looked forward to doing myself. My personal motto is "keep Fridays free." If something comes up that I want to do, I have the luxury of doing it! A last-minute meeting, shopping for clothes, or heading up to the lake for an early start to the weekend? Cool!

I have dedicated myself to working while my kids are at school Monday through Thursday. My personal morning routine gets handled before diving into work, so I know not to schedule anything before 10:00 a.m. On Mondays, I have a standing 10:30 a.m. meeting with my business partner Claire and our project manager. I don't allow anyone else to book appointments with me on Mondays. That makes a long weekend getaway easy. Monday is my day to sit down, catch up on emails, and prepare for the week.

Tuesday through Thursday, my work hours are 10:00 a.m. to 2:00 p.m. That's when I work on new content and programs. People can also schedule podcast episodes with me or meetings about upcoming opportunities for that time. That time frame on those three days is for anything and everything having to do with work. And I ensure that those hours are devoted to work and nothing personal. Since I have plenty of time before and after to take care of any personal responsibilities, this allows me to focus only on what is needed for my business.

This is my ideal weekly work schedule! Now it's your turn to design your dream week.

You must block off time on your calendar that's specifically allocated to work. But the magic is in designing your business around your ideal schedule. What are your ideal work hours? Specifically, which days of the week do you work? How many hours are you working a day? How much of your time is allocated to your family? How about your friends? Do you have personal time each day to fit in a workout or journaling? This is your opportunity to create your ideal scenario, so don't be shy about writing down exactly what you want.

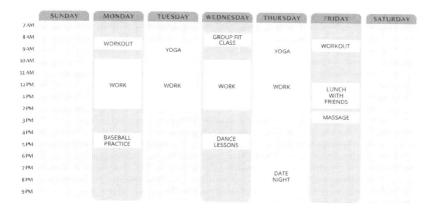

	SUNDAY	MONDAY	TUESDAY	WEDNESDAY	THURSDAY	FRIDAY	SATURDAY
7 AM							
8 AM		WORKOUT		GROUP FIT CLASS		WORKOUT	
9 AM			YOGA		YOGA		
10 AM							
11 AM							
12 PM		WORK	WORK	WORK	WORK	LUNCH WITH FRIENDS	
1 PM							
2 PM							
3 PM						MASSAGE	
4 PM		BASEBALL PRACTICE		DANCE LESSONS			
5 PM							
6 PM							
7 PM							
8 PM					DATE NIGHT		
9 PM							

PRO TIP

Reassess your schedule often. You may find that your ideal schedule shifts dramatically at different seasons of the year or of your life. Your summer hours and schedule may be vastly different than during the school year. Keep your calendar up to date and time blocked off where desired so you don't find yourself booked in inopportune times.

Risk-Taking

Entrepreneurship isn't for the faint of heart. It's not a get-rich-quick scheme. And it's not easy. It takes work, being consistent over a long period of time—and someone who is willing to take risks. It is not about taking crazy risks but calculated risks. You have to be willing to stretch a little and take chances to get the life you desire. **If you aren't willing to take a chance on yourself, why should you expect anyone else to take a chance on you?** If you refuse to try something new, how can you expect anything to change?

Einstein really said it best: "The definition of insanity is doing the same thing over and over again expecting a different result."

If you want a bigger and brighter reality for yourself, if you want to spend your life pursuing your purpose and your passions and you aren't already, then it's time to take chances.

Take a chance on your idea. Take a chance on doing the thing you have been hesitant to do, like going live on social media. Take a chance on hiring someone to help you. Take a chance on expanding your operations.

Remember, with every chance you take, it isn't a failure if it doesn't pan out just as you had hoped. Rather, it's a new lesson learned to help you reach your goals. This is a painfully beautiful reality of life.

Setting Boundaries

Setting boundaries helps you accomplish and enjoy more without burning out. Often, when we start our own business, we feel like we have to say yes to everything. Or maybe we're just a natural people pleaser and the word "yes" all too often comes out of our mouth.

You will soon realize you cannot do everything in your business (or life) and that therefore it's important to protect yourself and set boundaries. You must become okay with saying no to some things so you have the time and energy to say yes to the important things. If going to your daughter's school concert is important to you but you say "yes" to every business opportunity that comes your way, then you'll quickly find yourself missing the things that mean the most to you, leaving you feeling burnt out and unhappy.

Be warned: when you're just starting out, you'll find yourself saying yes to taking on more clients and yes to responding to questions and emails at all hours of the day. You can quickly find yourself in burnout mode, resenting both the work and the people you work with.

Write down your nonnegotiables, the things that you absolutely need to protect in your schedule, and then protect this space by blocking off time for them in your calendar. Only you can guard your time. Make your yeses count by saying no to anything that doesn't measurably get you closer to your dream life. Think about some of those things. What are the things you do that do not bring you joy and do not bring you closer to your dream life?

Attitude

You can and should be as intentional about your attitude as you are about your finances and work life. And attitude comes down to having the right mindset along with the right approach to failure.

Mindset

Mindset matters. The right mindset helps you push through the hardest days so you can stay motivated and focused to achieve what you set out to do. Having the right mindset will help you stay grounded and make the journey more enjoyable. On my mindset journey, I learned two important lessons that have helped me find joy and happiness while building my own business: the importance of flexibility + appreciation.

My first mindset coach, Brandon Barber, taught me the importance of having flexibility in the outcome and that having a strict blueprint for my dreams can be detrimental to happiness. When we have a strict blueprint and it doesn't turn out *exactly* to plan, we can easily set ourselves up for disappointment. Let's do an exercise Brandon did with me. Close your eyes (but first, read the next paragraph).

Imagine your dream home. What does the yard look like? How is the landscaping? Describe it. When you walk through the front door, what do you see? What do you smell? As you move through the entryway and into the kitchen, what does it look like? Now walk into the living room. You can imagine walking from room to room if you'd like, but these four areas alone are plenty for this exercise. Now close your eyes and picture what you see— everything from the color of the walls to the décor to the flooring and appliances. Maybe even speak what you envision out loud. Spare no detail. Imagine you are creating the blueprint.

When your dream home becomes your reality, it isn't going to look as perfect as you'd imagined. When you pictured the front lawn of your home, was the grass super green and lush? Well, if you have a dog, then the reality may look like brown spots where your dog has peed on your beautiful landscaping. The flower beds may have weeds, mosquitoes, or both. This is reality.

When you pictured your front entry, was it clean and clear? Or did you see a bunch of shoes strewn about near the door?

How about when you walked into your kitchen? I bet it looked immaculate. But the reality is there are likely dishes in the sink and papers and bills stacked in the nook in the corner. Reality isn't a perfect picture. Though it is essential to hold a vision, it is just as imperative to have flexibility in the outcome.

My second mindset coach, Brad Bizjack, taught me how to practice appreciation and enjoyment in the face of frustration and disappointment so I could achieve happiness right away versus having to wait until a big goal was met. There will absolutely be setbacks along the journey as it takes time to achieve our big goals and witness our dream life transforming into our reality.

Think about the dream life you are sketching out for yourself. There is a secret to reaching happiness sooner rather than later. If you must wait until all the boxes on your list are checked, you may be waiting a long time. After 10 years, I still haven't checked *all* the boxes on my list. (However, I am living my dream life as we speak, even if I don't have that beach house . . . yet.) Why? Because I have learned how to stop and appreciate every moment, both good and bad—and I am living life with purpose, gratitude, and appreciation every single day. Remind yourself of your progress and enjoy the dream life as it unfolds detail by detail along your journey.

I have also learned how to find gratitude in some of the most challenging moments and how to use the lessons to become a better businesswoman. Life outside the office often teaches us some of the greatest lessons to take back into it. For example, I have gratitude for my children even on the days when they test me to the max—and boy, are those days often! Every time we have a challenging moment, I find myself learning more about myself and them and appreciating those mini milestones. My daughter is a perfect example. When she was young, we recognized a pattern in her behavior: whenever she wouldn't get her way or she would get upset, she instantly started destroying things. One moment she would be fine and the next she would throw everything off the table and rip a book to pieces. We realized that her nature was to handle unfavorable situations and emotions in a reactionary way. This is insanely frustrating as a parent.

This was an opportunity for us to learn not only about her but also ourselves and, specifically, how to manage difficult situations. I can't say I have the magic answer—I'm not a parenting coach; I'm a business coach—but I learned to pause, understand more about her, pay attention to what triggers her, and try doing things to calm her before she goes from zero to a hundred in two seconds.

I also learned a lot about myself in those moments. I learned that when I don't know what's going on, I can also become reactive as well as defensive. Having these moments makes life less than perfect, but with a mindset trained to find gratitude and appreciation in everything, I can find the joy even in these unfavorable moments. Instead of seeing the glass as half empty, or trying to see it as half full, I look for a pitcher to fill up my cup. What a special gift to be able to understand my daughter more and help her cope through these moments so she can learn to work through her frustrations better. How grateful I am for these moments that teach me how to communicate with someone who is acting out of fear and frustration—especially when it's my daughter!

It's moments like these that help teach me how to address difficult situations in my business with a better, more effective approach. In your business, you will 100 percent interact with people who challenge you. However, what you learn day to day from them will impact how you function and grow in your business.

No matter how hard it gets in varying moments, enjoy the growth happening in you and everyone else involved.

To me, appreciating every little moment truly is magic because it puts you in your dream life *right now*. **You don't have to wait until you get your new car, your dream home, or a big financial break.** Start actively looking for how you can appreciate everything around you to start living in this brain space as often as possible and soon it will become a part of your reality.

Failure

Don't let failure hold you back. There will be many moments along your journey when you feel like you are failing in this process. When we don't reach our goals, we typically feel that way. Trust me: as an entrepreneur, you will fail many times. In fact, you should be concerned if you're not "failing."

Another important attitude shift is to redefine your definition of, and maybe even more importantly your relationship to, failure. What if failing didn't have to have such a negative connotation or impact on your mental state? What if you could change your mindset around failure so when you inevitably "fail" at a point along the journey, you don't experience sadness, frustration, or anger but instead feel hopeful and inspired?

If you are ready to release failure and the feelings around it whenever it happens, do this exercise with me (another Brandon Barber favorite). The brain can't tell a lie from the truth, so let's change your definition of failure to a definition that will mean you never experience failure as a negative. Failure, generally speaking, means a lack of success. In my mind, failure was any time I didn't reach a goal. With this definition, I often felt like a failure. Maybe you feel the same way. So instead, I want you to change the definition of failure.

Give it a try. Redefine what failure means to you.

When I did this exercise, I changed the definition to *failure is when I do not reach a goal and don't learn something in the process.*

With this new definition, I never feel like a failure because I *always* learn something in the process. Whether it's an unmet goal, a conversation that goes south, or a child acting out, I don't feel like a failed business owner, friend, or parent when I live within the parameters of *my* definition. I feel gratitude and appreciation for the challenge and the lesson I learned in the process. So too will your new definition allow you to change the way you view and treat your goals. And if you can't think of one, just use mine (it works!).

It's important to think long and hard about your dream life because you don't want to spend time, energy, and money on a path that's not leading you to the *lifestyle you desire.* In my sophomore year of college, I switched from a psychology major to the nursing program. I chose nursing because I liked helping people; I hadn't even considered the lifestyle I wanted! I found the human body fascinating, which made studying bearable. I also had a lot of choices in the type of work I could do as a nurse. It wasn't until I graduated that I realized how misaligned nursing was with my ideal dream life. The schedule wasn't flexible, and my $0.25-per-hour raise every year certainly wasn't going to fund my second home on the lake.

Situations like these are exactly why, before you create your offer, you start with identifying and visualizing your dream life and work scenario. Though there are strategies to make sure you are creating something someone will want to buy, your foremost goal should be to make sure it is aligned with the lifestyle you are trying to create. **The key is to design your work around your dream life, not your life around your work.** Write out your dream life, find pictures that illustrate it, and post the collage somewhere you'll see it every day and appreciate every little milestone you reach along the journey.

CHAPTER 2

THE FIRST OF THREE DECISIONS: WHAT WILL YOU SELL?

You've defined your dream life. *Great job!* The next step on the road to working efficiently to earn more with less effort and more enjoyment—to turn your passion, knowledge, and skills into a real, marketable offer—will require you to ask yourself three questions: (1) What will I sell? (2) What format will I use to present my content? and (3) What is my preferred payment model to increase my profits? Over time, you will be able to develop more than one offer, product, or service to create a product suite. But, as always, let's start at the beginning: concentrate on one offer you want to sell online.

Decide what to sell.

Just before I launched my most successful digital offer, I was sitting in my basement on the far end of my wraparound couch, snuggled deep into the corner, typing my little fingers away while my husband and children played beside me. I had been working on creating this new digital offering every chance I had for weeks. Then this feeling of panic came over me as I thought, "What if no one buys this? What if I spend all this time creating and no one wants it?"

Most entrepreneurs have harbored these same doubts. As self-doubt creeps in and you lose self-confidence, you begin to question everything. You wonder if this is a total waste of time. But because you have a passion for what you are doing and are clear about the dream life you want to create, you find the courage and conviction you need to keep moving forward.

I'm not sure this fear ever goes away; you simply get better at shushing the voice inside your head quicker to get back to work. It's the same fear my friend Stephanie shared with me six years after my first launch. As we sat across the table from each other and I dipped a tortilla chip into the guacamole, she said, "I don't know where to start, and what if no one buys what I put out there?"

Stephanie is a talented yoga instructor, and though she didn't want to stop teaching yoga in person, she did want to stop trading all her time for money. She wanted a digital offer she could sell to hundreds if not thousands of yogis while she was out on the back nine of a golf course with her husband trying to beat their personal best scores. I explained to Stephanie that the best way to come up with her first offer for people to buy is to ask her current community what they want. *If there is already a desire for something, it will be much easier to sell.*

I asked Stephanie, "Is there anything they are asking for that isn't being offered at the studio? Are they sharing any frustrations about not being able to attend in-person classes that could be solved with an online offer?"

Stephanie went to the streets (a.k.a. spoke with members of her yoga classes and private clients) to get some ideas. After visiting her mom 500 miles away and teaching a few yoga classes in her mom's neighborhood clubhouse, Stephanie received requests to come back to teach more classes. When she explained that she wasn't local, they asked for a video version they could stream into the clubhouse. It was in this moment that she created a plan for her first digital offer. The best part is that she already had a paying customer before she even created her offer! Simply by listening to the existing needs and desires of her students, Stephanie was able to hit a home run with her first offer.

Stephanie wasn't the first, and she definitely won't be the last, to have concerns that no one would find value in what she had to offer only to see that concern quickly diminish. I've seen someone successfully sell a course on mushrooms! And I've seen someone else sell a course on how to teach a horse to dance!

Someone will find value in your offer too. Your idea doesn't even have to be original. If it did, it would be like saying you could never open a gym because there are already gyms out there. You offer a uniqueness no one else does. You may target a different clientele, just like Planet Fitness and Lifetime Fitness—million-dollar gyms catering to two very different crowds—do. And there are many more successful fitness concepts in the market. In fact, if there are other successful people out there offering something like what you want to do, it just shows that they have proven there is demand. In a world of 7.8 billion people, I have no doubt that you can find enough people to buy your offers to be just as successful as those businesses, if not more.

Use these three preliminary questions to be bold and move forward to craft an offer that you are behind 100 percent. Being in action and finalizing a product or service you can offer is far more important than having the "perfect" offer. As you gain experience crafting offers, you'll gain confidence in the value of it and how to provide it.

Stephanie knew right away that she wanted to create digital yoga classes. You may not know what you want to offer yet or, if you already have an offer, what you want to offer next. The idea is taking what you know and feel passionate about (even if it is a product) and figuring out how to turn it into passive income—just like what Stephanie did. The following Turn Your Knowledge into Passive Income exercise I developed can help gain clarity around this. The goal is to identify the knowledge and skills you already possess that bring joy into your life that you could shape into a digital offer and sell.

Think about all the things you love to learn about. What are the books on your shelf? What podcasts do you listen to? What catches your eye or ear when you are out and about?

What do you find yourself talking about over and over again with friends, family, or colleagues? Is it travel? Working out? Cooking? Spirituality?

Think about the skills you have. And don't sell yourself short! You have a ton of skills. You probably just haven't viewed them as useful yet. Think of everything you are good at and enjoy. You may have developed skills from work or volunteer experiences or from anything you've ever done. If you need more paper, get some (see that mindset shift!). Once you have listed everything, circle the ones that make you happy and that you would love to offer, whether they're a product, teaching, coaching, or other service.

Here are some examples of skills and/or experience you may have that you otherwise may not have even thought of:

- organization
- cooking/baking
- writing
- taking direction
- social media
- creating graphics
- math
- cleaning
- fixing mechanical things
- working out
- marketing
- growing food and plants
- decorating and repurposing furniture
- taking pictures
- sales

Think about the goals you have accomplished already utilizing the things you love to learn or talk about or would love to teach. For example, maybe you've shed 50 pounds and want to teach people how to lose weight. Write down "losing 50 pounds" as an accomplishment. This can even go so far as being experienced with pregnancy! Let's say you have had four children and you know all the ins and outs of being pregnant—cravings, exercise, vitamins, false labor, and on and on. Well, guess what? You could coach other women who don't know what to expect or are fearful of their first pregnancy. These women have tons of questions you can answer!

Do you have 20 years' experience in financial planning? Write it down. Received a 200-hour yoga teacher certification and have taught over 300 yoga classes? Write it down. Successfully home-schooled two kids? Write it down. Traveled to 20+ countries? Write it down. No accomplishment or certification is too small. You will use these accomplishments to help show others that you are qualified to teach or otherwise help them. This will allow you to identify how you can stand out from your competition.

When do your neighbors, friends, and family come to you for help? For me, if I need math help, I'm calling my brother-in-law, a well-educated math teacher. If I have a question about sewing, I'm calling my childhood neighbor my mom always hired for hemming. If I have a landscaping question, I'm calling our family friend, a landscape engineer. If I have a security question, I'm calling my friend who worked for the secret service and ran security at multiple large corporations. If people already view you as the expert in a particular area, this might help you decide what to offer.

Taking all the information from the previous questions into consideration, which ideas come to mind for ways you could monetize your knowledge and skills? (You don't have to determine *how* to offer it yet; we will cover that in an upcoming chapter.)

If you already have a current audience, even just a few people, here are some more specific questions to help you discover what your next irresistible offer might be.

- What is your audience saying they want?
- What is the problem they report having?
- What is the solution or outcome they are looking for?

- What do they need in order to get what they want?
- Is there a way for you to provide a solution to their problem?
- How can you help give them what they want?

Sometimes, finding out what other people want is as plain as day because they ask you for it! "Do you have training on how to do handstands?" or "Do you have products that can help balance my hormones?" For example, my mother-in-law was sipping coffee and reading in a bookstore café when she saw an old acquaintance and the two started to catch up. The acquaintance said she had been asked by her boss to give a presentation at an important conference in her field, social work, but admitted that she felt unqualified and disoriented.

She asked if my mother-in-law knew anyone who could coach her on formulating and making the presentation. My mother-in-law said that she didn't, but she offered some helpful information from a book she had recently read and promised to email her friend if she thought of anyone who could serve as a good coach. For some history, my mother-in-law had given many public presentations and had thought about coaching before. But she thought she wasn't ready and that she needed to put together a brochure of her qualifications before she could make it "official." But when she got home, she realized that she could in fact help the other woman—brochure or no brochure—right now. She emailed her offering to help her acquaintance and gave her the price for four two-hour sessions. The woman was thrilled. It was a win-win!

Someone asked for something my mother-in-law was able to give, and she gave it. She had known for some time that she wanted to coach and had taken several seminars so that she felt qualified to provide it. She was ready to overcome her inner voice that was telling her she had to be "more" ready and abandon her self-doubts and just do it.

Sometimes it's a little more subtle, but people will inherently share their desires with you all the time. Your job is to listen. Listen for words such as "I wish" or "I would love." "I wish I could find more time to cook healthy meals!" This means they want to cook healthy meals at home but their challenge is time. Therefore, the need is for healthy meal recipes that can be prepared quickly. Here's how you introduce your offer: healthy meals that take less than 10 minutes to prepare. This could be sold as an e-book or a minicourse.

Sometimes the "wants" also come in the form of complaints: "I hate" or "XYZ feels so hard." These are the moments when you can use your knowledge and skills to make people's lives so much better. Maybe you've had experience navigating certain situations before and found the perfect solutions that you can now share.

"I hate that my prepregnancy clothes don't fit anymore!" They want to fit into their pre-baby clothes. Their challenge is losing weight post-baby. Your solution could be meal-replacement shakes that others have had success with, or you could provide a fitness program to help them lose weight. This could be in the form of a prerecorded workout series you offer.

Once you have an idea of what you would be excited about offering and what you want your purchasers to be able to accomplish, you need to get laser focused on all the information you will want to include. I like to brain-dump onto Post-it notes because it allows me to move things around easily.

Here is an example of fleshing out content for a gardening course with the Post-it notes.

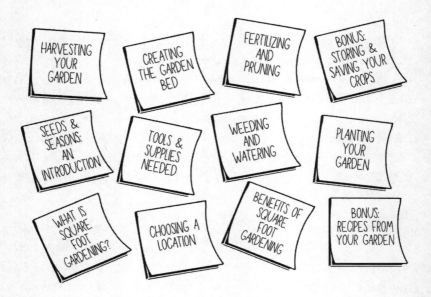

You can then clump the items together and turn them into modules, phases, or steps in your offer. They may become lessons in a course or could become multiple products in a product suite. You may arrange these topics according to chronological or some other order:

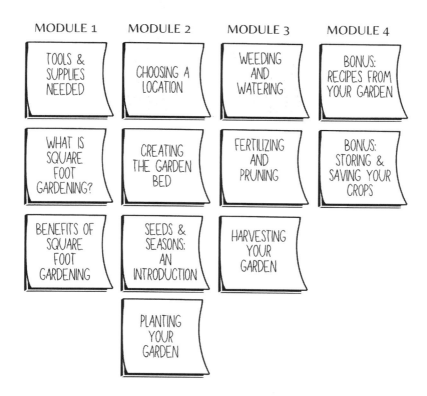

Product Suites

You may come up with several ideas for your offer (I hope that you do!). The good news is you can turn these ideas into multiple offers, which will collectively become your product suite. After all, no one said we have to stop at one offer! They could be a collection of physical products, digital products or services, or one-on-one coaching.

Sometimes a product suite is sequential with a clear progression from start to finish. Take the following as an example:

Other times, a product suite is nonsequential, meaning you could bring customers in at varying points with different offers, such as the following:

In a nonsequential product suite, someone could first buy yoga accessories and then your advanced yoga program. Or someone could first purchase your inversion workshop and then decide to buy the yoga accessories you promote.

There is no right or wrong answer. What is important is that your offers all be aligned with what your audience wants. This allows you to turn one-time customers into lifetime customers in the most efficient way possible. Your additional offers can also turn into great upsells or downsells (more on this later). Developing an entire product suite takes time. It's something I have been slowly developing over the past four years. Don't let the product suite overwhelm you; let it inspire you to see all the ways you can generate revenue for your business over time. All I want you to focus on now is deciding what *one* offer can be.

Consider selling an offer through affiliate marketing.

Affiliate marketing is when you sign up to be an ambassador for another person or company's product, service, or offer by referring others who buy their offer. You can always consider using affiliate marketing as a second offer that would promote someone else's product/offer as a part of your own product suite. When customers use your referral link to purchase, you receive compensation in the form of money or free products. Affiliate marketing dates back to the 1940s when some of the first direct-sales businesses were formed using referral marketing instead of employing sales associates.

In recent years, many companies outside direct-sales companies (e.g., Target, Sephora, and Amazon) have jumped onboard with affiliate marketing and are not just reserving this opportunity for big influencers with large followings. Anyone can create affiliate accounts. In addition to big companies providing commissions when selling their products, many coaches and digital creators offer affiliate commissions when you promote and sell their courses or programs. Software is another industry that often has affiliate programs, among many others.

This is one of my favorite ways to expand offerings and bring in extra revenue because, as an affiliate, the work from you is directed toward marketing, not creating or delivering the product or offer. That means you can start promoting and earning money almost instantly. The key to making this a successful additional revenue stream is to promote products or services that you truly believe in, that are aligned with you and your business, and that will benefit your customers. Oftentimes, these are products or services that you personally use or with which you are quite familiar. We have served as an affiliate to refer people to physical products, digital courses, digital templates, programs, and software and have an entire page on our website dedicated to the tools and offers we stand by and promote. Not everything we promote offers affiliate partnerships that allow us to earn income from sales, but many do. From our website, our customers access other companies' products that we promote with a referral link, thereby ensuring that we are paid for the referral.

Think about whether affiliate offers are for you. Do you want to establish another revenue stream without creating your own offer or something new? Do you find value in someone else's product or offer and want to receive compensation for promoting it? Have you found a product, an offer, or software that will help your clients with their transformations? Do you mind not having control over the deliverables?

Later, I will ask you more questions to help you flesh out your offers even more, but for now, the idea is to just get some ideas flowing on what topics would give you joy and purpose digitally. After addressing how to present your offer and how to think about what and how to charge, we will then turn to how to increase efficiency to make money while you sleep, so you can turn your dream life into a reality.

CHAPTER 3

THE SECOND OF THREE DECISIONS: WHAT PRODUCT FORMAT WILL YOU USE?

You have your dream life in mind and have identified what you want to offer. Now let's explore various formats you can use to sell your content. There are many ways you can bundle the knowledge and skills you offer the world. You can expect to generate more revenue if you create multiple products, possibly in various formats, for a suite of products. But let's not get ahead of ourselves. Start with what you decided to sell in chapter 2 and let's decide which format will work best for that offer. No matter what you decide to sell, it's important to think about the time and resources it will take to create and support your customers. Ask yourself, "Is this aligned with the business and lifestyle I am trying to create?"

I coach Amelia Forczak, one of my superstars and a highly sought-after ghostwriter and book coach who came to me saying that she wanted to spend more time with her young daughter but felt completely maxed out running her business. Her company, Pithy Wordsmithery, specializes in offering extensive one-on-one support to authors. They assist with outlining, writing, editing, self-publishing, and marketing—all while working closely with clients. This one-on-one format isn't bad—in fact, it works quite well—but it's rooted in trading time for money. If Amelia wanted to generate more revenue without sacrificing time with her daughter, she would need to either hire more team members to take on more clients or increase her prices—or, better yet, create a digital offer she could scale.

As we worked together to create her digital offer and automate more of her business, she found herself at a pivotal moment. Amelia had arrived at our coaching session with an entire list filled with the content she was going to provide every month for her membership. After she got through telling me everything she was going to do, I reminded her that she had come to me saying she wanted to free up her time, not add more to her plate. I asked her how much time and effort it was going to take her every month to prepare and support her community in this way.

She paused for a minute and then, with disappointment in her voice, responded, "Too much time."

She went back to the drawing board and created a digital offer that went beyond the one-on-one support format, thinking she could make more money with less of her time. Her first digital offer, called So You Want to Write a Book?, is a minicourse that covers everything she would tell new clients within the first two to three hours of one-on-one consulting. Using video lessons and worksheets, she found a way to walk clients through the process digitally so that she could share the information at scale without it taking any more of her time. She quickly gained positive feedback from aspiring authors who loved the course and got a lot of value out of it—even without the one-on-one support.

After experiencing that success, she decided to rethink her membership idea to add value in a time-efficient way and founded the Authors' Club, which is a low-cost monthly membership that is rooted in community, empowerment, and education. Members meet virtually every two weeks for an Ask Me Anything group coaching session as well as a live writing session during which everyone turns off their mic and camera and writes together from afar. There's also a Facebook group where members can get to know one another and build a support network for their book launches.

Aspiring authors have shared rave reviews about both programs, and Amelia is thrilled that she has found a way to continue growing her business without sacrificing her work-life balance. This is just one example how a change in format can make all the difference in the world.

As I break down different formats, keep your dream life in mind. You always want to choose a format that best fits the time, effort, energy, resources, and money it's going to take to get it up and running to support your customers. The following are some of the most common formats.

One-on-One Support

Coaching, teaching, or writing one-on-one is a very high-touch, personalized offer. But it is also the least scalable. With one-on-one support, someone pays you for your undivided attention and individualized support. This may take more time than many of the other ways you could offer content because you are meeting with one person at a time. On the upside, you can charge a higher price for the one-on-one since it is individualized support. After all, your time is valuable.

One way to make your one-on-one support more efficient is by combining it with a course. Such a course can teach the basics and then, when you have your one-on-one sessions, you can dive deeper. When I first started this type of coaching and consulting, I spent a lot of time teaching the basics of building a website and earning revenue with digital offers. After taking on a few clients, I came to the realization that I was teaching them all the same thing—which was incredibly inefficient. Over time, I turned the basic knowledge into lessons and packaged it up as a course. I could then assign my private clients "homework" to watch the lessons and then they would come prepared to make quicker progress on their websites and businesses. It was a win-win for us both.

To determine whether one-on-one support is right for you, ask yourself:

- How much time will it take to prepare for the sessions?
- How long will the sessions be?
- How much time will be required to spend after each session to deliver what I promise?
- Am I providing a recording or notes I need to prepare afterward?
- Where will I put this content?
- Do I have someone who could help me upload this content to save me time?
- How much should I charge for my time so I don't end up resenting my client?

Once you factor in how much time it will take you to prepare for the session, then conduct the actual session, and finally the time after, what are you earning hourly? Is that enough?

But, as always, it's about more than money. Aside from the time it takes and the money earned, does one-on-one support light you up? Do you look forward to having individual time with clients? If the answer is yes, if you can manage the time commitment, and if the earnings feel good, then maybe one-on-one support is for you.

Workshops, Masterclasses, Webinars

These formats are a bit different than a one-on-one in that they offer just a quick one-and-done training or experience with you. Some people think that workshops, masterclasses, and webinars are synonymous with each other, but I would disagree. I consider a workshop to entail less teaching *at* your attendees and more interactive work to achieve the purpose of the workshop, whereas a masterclass or webinar provides a place to come listen and learn, and the attendees process what they learned more after they leave. All three can be prerecorded or live. They could be 15 minutes to four-plus hours in length. You can charge for these offers or use them as free trainings to sell other offers.

To determine whether workshops, masterclasses, or webinars are for you, ask yourself:

- Will this be the best way to present the information and give my audience value?

- Do I need to host this live in order to be able to interact with people, or can I do it in a way that will allow me to prerecord it? (Though prerecording your training can eliminate a lot of stress and allow you to hold the training at any time, there will likely be a bit more excitement from your audience when it's held live. You can also gain new insights into your audience and their needs when the events are held live, and everyone is able to ask questions and interact.)

PRO TIP

Beware of trolls when you are on live. These are the people who just say nasty things in the comments to throw you off your game. Have a helper with you to kick these people out so you can focus on the training.

- Can it be offered all year long or is it seasonal? In other words, can it only be promoted at certain times of the year? (For example, a training on trimming your Christmas tree will be best during the winter holiday season. A workshop on back-to-school wellness will be the most effective at the end of summer vacation as families prepare to head back to school. Seasonal offerings will limit the time you can offer them, but they can also create an influx of sales. By being hyper focused on what is relevant during a particular season, they create a natural urgency to buy the offer then. People feel like they *need* it now!)

Courses

Courses are typically a series of prerecorded training or teaching videos that help clients reach a transformation through your "process." Think about a course you may have attended in school where you trained, learned, and implemented. Your customers will do the same. You can structure your course any way you want as well as provide worksheets, text to read, and even guided support.

Your digital course could be as short as five lessons or as extensive as 50 or more. This format is incredibly scalable due to its minimal individual attention. The bulk of your workload on this type of offer will be on the front end, creating the course and providing ongoing marketing efforts to continue to get new customers in order to gain additional revenue. We talk about ways to make your marketing more efficient in chapter 7.

If digital courses are an avenue you want to explore, I recommend providing your content to three one-on-one coaching clients or a small group to get individual feedback and help you test and improve it. Though one-on-one coaching might not be in your long-term plan, it can help you create a course that achieves a quick client transformation.

To determine whether a course is for you, ask yourself:

- Do you want to create a training once and reuse it repeatedly?
- Do you want a more hands-off model to teach many?
- Will the transformation you want to promise be achievable in this format?

Communities

Another common format is a community, where you can give people access to other people who share common interests. These can stand alone (e.g., a grief community) or complement your main offer (e.g., a place for customers of your product to interact). Your community could be a group of people with the same goal, people who are working through the same steps, or people who are like-minded in some other way. However, to be successful, your community will need a purpose.

You can offer a community through a Facebook group, a community space on your website, or a special app specifically for communities. Keep in mind that where you host it may or may not allow you to automate the admission process. For example, if you host your community on Facebook but take payment through your website, you or the customer will need to manually add themselves to the group, whereas if your community space is hosted on your website, granting access can be automated to occur upon purchase of your offer.

You could offer monthly Q&A sessions through your community or add new training materials there for each member to access. You can offer as much or as little as you want, but the way you set up your community and what you offer them will determine how much time and effort it will take you to support it. Therefore, be mindful of the time you have to devote to this format and set up your community accordingly. If you want to spend less time with it, create a culture where members help each other so you are not the only one providing support. Another way to reduce your time in this way is to hire help.

When we started our community for GROworkspace, we encouraged everyone in the community to support one another. This took the pressure off me to have to be the one to help everyone and answer all their questions. Eventually, we hired an administrator to manage the group, which allowed me to only spend about one hour a month on my direct support for the community group.

One way in which communities can be especially lucrative is that they typically require ongoing support. This means that this format is ripe for a subscription payment model.

To determine if a community is for you, ask yourself:

- Is community something my clients need in order to accomplish their transformation?
- Is it something they desire?
- Does the subscription payment model work well for me and my customers?
- Does the time commitment work with my desired lifestyle?

Templates

With a templates format, your customers don't have to start from scratch. They will become familiar with the templates and easily be able to reuse them again and again. This is more efficient for you than working with your customers one-on-one, and it saves customers time and money in achieving their goals whether the templates are used by themselves or to supplement one-on-one or course formats. For example, our clients want to create websites and digital offers as fast as possible. As such, we offer pre-made templates, including copywriting templates, website page design templates, and graphic templates, all of which help speed up the process of our clients creating their websites, offers, and marketing materials.

Typically, templates are a one-time payment purchase, but you can also turn them into a membership / subscription payment model if you are uploading new templates for your clients to use on a regular basis. Pre-built resources and templates on a subscription service were essentially the business model we used to generate $3.5 million in four years through our first brand.

To determine whether templates are for you, ask yourself:

- Do my clients need something that prevents them from starting from scratch?
- Will providing a template help speed up their ability to achieve the transformation?
- Do templates make sense for my line of work?

Group Programs

Group programs provide a way for you to serve more than one person at a time, allowing you to instantly maximize your efforts beyond one-on-one coaching. In a group program, your clients look to you as a leader to teach them. This is different from a mastermind group where all the members share with each other—as they are themselves all leaders. Be sure to label your offer appropriately as either a mastermind or group program.

Instead of five individual one-on-one sessions, you can have one session where all five students meet. Besides the fact that it saves you time, students often learn from others in these group settings as well. For example, our Build a Blissful Business students frequently attend live group coaching sessions and afterward reveal that they got so much clarity about their own offer by watching us work with other students.

Your group program can present your content in as few or as many formats as you want. Determine what you need to include to help group members reach their goals and then determine how many people you can effectively serve in this way. As with your analysis of every format, determine how much time it will take you to create this content and to adequately support your group members.

Typically, a group program would use the one-time payment or payment-plan model.

To determine whether a group program is for you, ask yourself:

- Would I prefer a one-to-many experience?
- Will my customers benefit from witnessing others working through the same process?

Each of these formats offers something different for both you and your students/clients. Remember, the long-term goal is to build a product suite and have as many offers as you'd like, using as many or as few formats as you want to generate multiple streams of revenue. But before you decide on your first offer or format, consider the information in the next chapter about payment models.

PRO TIP

Keep it simple with a clear path. Start with one offer with a goal to expand to three to five. Avoid making offers just to make offers. Remember that you have to manage them all (or your team does). You can have a TON of success with just a few.

CHAPTER 4

THE THIRD OF THREE DECISIONS: WHAT PAYMENT MODELS WILL FIT YOUR DREAM LIFE AND MAXIMIZE PROFITS?

The way you charge for your offers can completely change your business model. And since you are designing your business around your desired lifestyle, it's an important factor to consider. The following are just a few of the many different types of payment models you may want to consider.

Types of Payment Models

One Offer, One Payment

Commonly referred to as a "pay in full" option, this is when you sell something for a one-time-only payment. The advantage of this payment model is that you get all your money up front. The disadvantage is that in order to make money the next week or month to keep your business alive, you need to put the workshop on again or create another workshop. At a minimum, if you keep the same workshop and sell a prerecorded version, you will need to keep finding people to buy that workshop. Otherwise, you will need to expend more time and energy to find other ways to support yourself, presumably with other digital offers.

A one-time payment is a simple transaction that can make you a lot of money, but you will constantly need to find new customers or have more things for them to purchase in order to generate more income.

Advantages

➤ You earn all the money up front.

Disadvantages

➤ You must make additional sales to keep generating revenue.

One Offer, Multiple Payments

Rather than earning a large sum of money up front and nothing thereafter, you may prefer to spread the payment over a longer period, getting less money initially but at a more consistent rate for several months. If this appeals to you, you can structure one offer but with a payment plan. This is different from a subscription because a subscription requires there be ongoing content for ongoing payments. One advantage of this is that more people will be able to accept your offer because they don't need to cover the whole cost immediately. These multiple payments are simply the one-time price, with whatever additional amount you might add, split up over time, with a clear ending date.

A second advantage to a multiple-payment plan is that you can collect slightly more because you are delaying collection of the entire price. It's common to add an extra 10 to 30 percent to the purchase price when someone pays with a payment plan versus paying all up front. You can pick a higher price for your offer and then offer a discount for receiving payment in full upon purchase. This strategy encourages your buyer to pay in full rather than paying a higher price, yet it gives an option for those who can't pay in full to purchase at a lower initial price point.

The disadvantage of a one-time offer with multiple payments is that there is the inherent risk that you never get your full purchase price. Since customers have already obtained 100 percent of your offer, people may at some point decide to just quit paying. Requiring them to sign an ACH agreement authorizing their bank to make the payments as scheduled is a good way to avoid that situation as it's more difficult for them to stop paying (although they can always contact the bank and revoke their authorization for automatic payments to you). Just bear in mind that this lack of payment may have nothing to do with you or the value of your offer. Their personal financial circumstances may have changed, causing them to tighten their budgets. Or their personal career goals and interests may have changed so they don't feel that they need your offer anymore. In these circumstances, they will be more likely to stop paying or pester you to try to get you to stop collecting or, in some cases, even to refund amounts already paid. Knowing that they haven't paid in full yet, they may psychologically become very demanding and want more from whatever your offer has provided them.

The fact that you may have drawn in more customers by offering a payment plan may make it worthwhile to have some of these collection problems. Another possible solution to this problem is to consider an option where content is "dripped" out over the course of the payment plan. For example, if you offer a six-month payment plan, you can restrict access to the course and only release part of the course each month until all content is released in month six. There are many creative ways to do this— your way won't be right or wrong but rather an opportunity to test, evaluate, and adjust.

Advantages

> You can sign up more people, thereby making it more accessible.

> You can charge more and make more money.

Disadvantages

> They may stop paying.

Recurring Income

As for me and my business, I knew I wanted to maximize profits through recurring income. Recurring payments can come from monthly auto-shipping, affiliate marketing commissions, or ongoing subscriptions or memberships. Recurring income will keep growing as long as your customers continue to buy. This income will compound as you continue to get new customers. You could bring in 10 customers in a month who keep ordering every month and the next month bring in 10 more customers who order every month and so on. If you did that every month and your customers continued to pay you, you would have 120 people paying you every month by the end of year one. This goes for anything that is sold with a recurring payment.

The realization that this sort of payment was for me hit me one ordinary summer day when I was walking outside to get the mail and a light bulb went off in my mind as bright as the sun in the sky. I'd expected to find a usual stack of junk mail, but as I flipped through the different envelopes and fliers, I noticed an official-looking envelope that was marked with hardly anything other than my name. It looked like a letter I'd received the month before with a paycheck inside from the direct-sales company I was representing. I hadn't made any sales that month like I had in the month prior, so I was confused. I opened the envelope and found a check for $108.78. *But how could it be a paycheck? I didn't sell anything that month.* This was the moment when I learned about recurring income. I realized I could either have many customers with one-time purchases or earn the same amount of money from fewer customers by leveraging a recurring-income stream.

Little did I know at the time that this "ah-ha" moment would be the start of a multi-million-dollar business. It's an important concept to understand, and, thankfully, it's one of the simpler ones. Sit back with your drink of choice (mine's a passion-fruit margarita, no salt, please!), and let's dive in so you can determine whether what you have in your business is a one-time payment strategy or a recurring-payment strategy. (Please just be sure not to drink too many margaritas while reading this chapter, as I don't want you to miss the bonus strategy where I will teach you how you can turn your one-time payments into recurring payments!)

Before launching our first product offering, it hit me that the check that showed up at my house when I didn't think I had sold anything was the secret to building more income with less effort. That $108 check was from having been involved in direct sales, a business model that revolves around recurring or residual income.

It's the idea that you bring in customers to your business and earn a commission on what they continue to purchase each month. You have an incentive to have your customers keep purchasing regularly. Auto-ship programs and discounted prices or rewards or bonuses for purchasing every month accomplish exactly this. When your customers sign up for this type of program, as long as they keep ordering, you keep earning money.

Direct-sales companies aren't the only ones that use these strategies. For example, I can sign up for an auto-shipment for my dog food every month to get a better price. Why do companies do this? It ensures that I keep buying from them, never stopping at a different pet shop for a bag of food. Recurring income results not just from repeat business but also from regularly repeating business.

This format works very well with consumable products. When I was heavily in direct sales, the company I promoted sold consumable wellness products. It was easy to get people to commit to auto-ship because the products they used and loved would run out and they would need more, so setting up automatic monthly orders made good sense. Instead of having to remember to order, the products would come right to their door every month.

When Claire and I had the idea for GROworkspace, it was originally an offer for a one-time purchase of a digital product with full payment in advance (the first format I mentioned earlier in the chapter). It was a digital course that taught Young Living Brand Partners how to build their direct-sales businesses. Thinking about that $108 check, I set about figuring out how to go beyond one-time offers, with or without multiple payments, and increase recurring payments. As I crafted our next offering, I asked myself, "What could I do to get someone to want to pay us every single month?"

This one question changed our entire business model and allowed us to generate $1 million in 20 months and over $3 million in four years.

Recurring Payments through Memberships and Subscriptions

GROworkspace offers a variety of premade content, templates, and training in the form of a membership/subscription model to serve the Young Living community. After first considering a one-time offer with one payment, we decided to offer editable templates and other resources such as small trainings and graphics to support a monthly subscription that would automatically renew every month unless canceled. The subscription would entitle subscribers to receive new content every single month, which they could then use to market their businesses. To further encourage subscriptions, we offered our original business training course for free when customers signed up for the subscription to get new monthly content.

This program offered our new customers memberships in our program by paying a monthly or annual subscription to continue taking advantage of our services (with us creating new essential-oils classes and monthly newsletters for them) and resources (training on how to market the class). As long as they remained subscribers, we continued to earn money from them for new content we added each month.

In month one, we made $8,000. Month two started to compound as only a few canceled and many more signed on and we made $20,000. Over subsequent months, it continued to grow and grow to a multi-million-dollar business.

If you like the idea of this model, think about how you could offer the ongoing content or support needed to have a subscription-based offer. Just be mindful of the time and effort it will take to follow through. Imagine you're teaching golf skills. You could start a membership program to include a community aspect, wherein your members would then pay you every single month to be a part of this "community," and in return for their payment, they would receive certain benefits such as being able to ask for, and receive, regular tips on golfing and getting feedback on their performance. Your members could each share a short video of their golf swing for you to review and provide them with feedback on their technique.

With this hypothetical membership model, you would have to spend a certain amount of time with each person to review their swing and their videos and provide valuable feedback. This is a scenario in which it would be very difficult to have a community of 5,000 people unless you hired an entire team of golf pros to review golf swings and give their feedback.

The cost of a membership will be based on the number of people you can have in your program. A higher price will likely lower the number of members who sign on, but having fewer people at a higher price may yield you the same amount of money. For example, you could charge $10 a month for 1,000 people and generate $10,000 a month in revenue, or you could have 100 people paying $100 a month and generate the same amount. It just depends on which would work better for what you want to provide. With our GROworkspace business, our motto was "the more, the merrier!" We were aiming for thousands and therefore started our membership at only $4.95 a month.

If your customers need continued support or content, a membership program makes sense. If you decide to do a membership, you may want to consider providing an annual rate, which would be beneficial for both you and the members. You get a larger lump sum up front, which could help with finances, and they will have committed to being a part of your membership for one year. Committing for a year will provide them with ample time to get what they need to experience the transformation you provide.

It is also common to give customers a discount—such as one month free—if they pay for the year up front. You don't have to do this, but it is something else to consider. A bonus or freebie could work just as well. For example, Amelia, the ghostwriter I mentioned previously, offers her minicourse for free when customers sign up for her membership and pay for the year up front versus paying every month.

In order to determine which approach you want, ask yourself these questions:

1. Do I want the larger sum up front?
2. Is it more beneficial for customers to initially sign up for more than a month at once?

Remember, your business is unique, and you have to decide what the best option is for you and your customers.

Advantages
➢ It results in more revenue with fewer customers than one-time offers.

Disadvantages
➢ You usually have to provide ongoing support or new content to get people to want to stay and not cancel.
➢ You have to manage failed payments.

Recurrent Payments from Affiliate Programs

Another way of receiving recurring income with very little work on your part is through the affiliate programs we discussed in the previous chapter. To maximize your income, look for affiliate programs that offer ongoing commission for recurring payments. For example, as a Kajabi affiliate, I earn income every month from the customers I have sent to Kajabi, which provided me with a referral or affiliate link that I use to promote their website-hosting platform. When people use my affiliate link to sign up to use their software, I receive a 30 percent commission. Yes, it's that simple! If the people I refer continue to pay Kajabi to use their software, I get a commission. And use of the software is usually long term. Every time Kajabi receives a payment from someone who used my Kajabi affiliate link, I receive a payment.

Advantages

➤ It's another revenue stream without you having to create the offer.

➤ You don't have to manage product delivery or customer support.

Disadvantages

➤ The company you promote could stop their affiliate-marketing program at any time, eliminating the revenue stream.

➤ Since sales are going through the other companies' software (payment processor and email system), it's harder to know who is buying from your community and what they are buying in order to retarget them with other offers.

Changing or Combining Formats and/or Payment Models

The formats I've mentioned in this chapter are not mutually exclusive. Another option for increased profitability is to combine your methods of payment. You could start with a one-time payment and, after customers consume the offer, they may need ongoing support. This could be your opportunity to pitch them a membership offering.

Our students often buy our Build a Blissful Business program to help them establish their brands, get their websites set up, create their first funnels to grow their email lists, and use automation to turn their leads into customers. They pay a one-time cost to get lifetime access to the training but only get support from us and our coaches for a limited time. Once they're done with the program, they often seek support in growing and expanding their businesses. It makes perfect sense for us to have a membership option that continues to support previous students on their ongoing business journey, where they can continue to ask us questions and get feedback on any content they are working on.

Take, for example, one of our clients, Kristina, who turned her in-person, one-on-one literacy-coaching business into an online course with prerecorded trainings. She had a course for teachers and a course for parents to help build successful readers and soon realized that parents would benefit from ongoing support as their children were learning to read. She has taken that information and now plans to offer a membership or subscription-model service for parents to receive ongoing support where they can ask questions as needed in a community forum. It will likely be a seamless transition and should work very well for her.

Think about a customer of yours. If you put together a one-time offer, would they need continued support after they complete that offer through a membership/subscription format?

Advantages

> ➤ You increase your revenue without acquiring new customers.
> ➤ You provide ongoing support for your customers to help get them even better results.

Disadvantages

> ➤ You have to create additional offers.

Decide What to Charge

You will constantly hear from coaches and influencers that you should charge what you are worth! But the problem with this is you can't *really* put a price on your worth because your worth is infinite. Or you may have a limiting belief that your worth is low. Instead of just blindly trying to come up with what you are "worth," use this guide to help you determine the best price for your offer.

1. What is the value of the transformation you are promising?
2. What do you need to charge to make a profit?
3. What are your competitors charging?
4. Do you want to be priced below or above them?
5. What do you need to charge so you don't end up resenting your customers?

After you get through those preliminary questions, it's time to dive deeper into your offer and ask yourself some questions.

1. How much is my offer?

2. Is it something anyone can easily purchase with pay-in-full, or will I sell more by offering a payment plan?

3. How do I need to provide support to my members in order to help them realize a transformation? Can it be in a way that is hands-off, such as a prerecorded training everyone would watch, or do I need to have one-on-one time with someone providing feedback? (Anytime you're providing individualized feedback, you can increase the cost of your services.)

4. How many people can I serve solo? If I want to serve more people, whom might I need to hire to allow my customers or members to have continued success? (We will get to hiring and outsourcing later in chapter 9. These are just questions to help you start to think about how you could offer your knowledge, skills, and services in a scalable way.)

The payment option(s) you choose should be in line with the dream life you want to create. Which model supports the lifestyle you want to live? My answer is to build multiple offers for multiple revenue streams to avoid putting all your eggs in one basket with a variety of payment options that can be fully automated offers for recurring income.

If your goal is to build your business to the point where you're working less than 10 hours a week, then you may need to go with an option that includes prerecorded or pre-created offerings that take your time only while you're creating them and then can be used over and over again. But you can also go with the option that includes an individualized model that requires you to spend time with each person or live trainings and offerings requiring you to show up repeatedly. However, if you want to work less than 10 hours a week, then you need to be prepared to hire support. For us, we chose to focus on a subscription model so we could generate a recurring-income stream to start. Then we expanded into one-time payment offers and then larger offers with payment plans. To do so, we hired content creators to free up more of our time so we could focus on expanding our offers to have a complete product suite with multiple offers and multiple payment options.

Now that you have an idea of how to determine what to sell, what format to use, and what payment options there are, it's time for some inspiration! Here are several examples of businesses and product suites that generate income with varying offers and payment programs:

As previously discussed, our original business, GROwork-space, offers a variety of premade content, templates, and training in the form of a membership/subscription model to serve Young Living Brand Partners. And though we began by charging $4.95 a month, we were able to increase it to $14.95 by month four. We also were able to grow our membership to 6,000 paying subscribers and $1 million in revenue in just 20 months and a total of over $3 million in four years.

Brenda Winkle is an educator, speaker, healer, coach, and guide who helps sensitive and successful high performers find, reclaim, and live from their full embodied YES through a variety of methods including breathwork.[1] Brenda was a music educator for 26 years with her master's in educational leadership. She became trained as an advanced trauma-informed breathwork facilitator and trauma-informed reiki master and is certified and highly trained in multiple energy-healing modalities.

Brenda's business comprises three offers:

1. One-on-one healing and breathwork sessions through a package called "Heal to the Yes" that is sold as a single session for $500 or a six-month package with 24 sessions for $9,000.

2. A group offer called "Yes Academy" that includes recorded modules, weekly breathwork sessions exclusive to the Yes Academy community, content calls, hot seats with somatic healing/coaching, and two one-on-one sessions every six months. Yes Academy is a six-month package that sells for $7,500.

3. Heal Yes Retreats are offered two times per year and include daily breathwork and training in energy-healing modalities such as reiki. They have been sold in the past for $3,500 but will increase to $7,000 in 2024.

Brenda offers payment-plan options in addition to pay-in-full. The price increases by $500 when someone chooses a payment-plan option. These offers helped her yield $21,600 in one month with an ongoing monthly income of $1,300 for five additional months due to the payment-plan option.

Stephanie Lombardo, founder of Flippin Empire, is a real-estate agent with an investment portfolio based on investing in real estate and renovating and renting homes. She decided to build a group program to teach other agents to do the same. She uses a group model with pre-built courses coupled with group coaching. She offers this with one-time and payment-plan options. With some coaching, she was able to generate over $5,000 with her new digital offer in just a couple months.

Celia Aris, a former COO of tech and wellness startups, is running a multiple six-figure business that supports entrepreneurs through a group program, membership, one-on-one coaching, and private consulting. Her Grown Ass Business program is an eight-week group program that includes community support and one-on-one support coaching. Once her students are done with the group program, she offers ongoing support in her membership with weekly accountability and continued support from her team. Her revenue is generated with 30 percent from her group program, 10 percent from her membership, and 40 percent from her one-on-one offers, with the rest coming from consulting and speaking.

CHAPTER 5

IDENTIFY YOUR IDEAL CUSTOMER

As I walked into the dining room one weekday afternoon, I noticed George, my father-in-law, hunched over with his elbows on the sun-splashed table and hands folded together over his tablet, just thinking. I asked what he was working on, and he said, "I'm thinking about who I can reach out to and pitch this opportunity. I want to go for the low-hanging fruit." It was a phrase he said often in our business conversations. As someone who ran businesses for 40+ years, he knew a thing or two about acquiring customers. Every time he said the phrase "low-hanging fruit," I pictured an apple tree with apples dispersed throughout, some on the highest branches that would require a tall ladder to get them and some on the lowest branches where I could reach up to grab the apples without assistance. It's as if the ones down low had been placed right in front of my face, begging to be plucked.

What George meant by "low-hanging fruit" was that he wanted customers who were easy to get—customers who didn't need much convincing and were ready and willing to buy what he had to sell. He wanted it to be as effortless as possible. He also wanted to find people who would return often, buy again and again, and refer others to him.

If you miss some of the key features of your ideal customer, it will cost you a lot of time, stress, and money. When done right, you will find selling to be at worst effortless and at best joyous. You are no longer scared to "sell" to people because there is no convincing anyone to buy. People are asking you for your offer. Sales become easier, your conversion rates become higher, your customer interactions become more enjoyable, and your revenues increase.

Now that you have identified your offer, you need to identify who will be interested in buying it before you figure out how to market it. Most people want to market their product to the broadest possible group of people, thinking that will get them more customers and make them more money. However, your ideal customer is more likely to buy your product with less effort on your part than all other potential customers. They will be a joy to work with, and they will be more likely to become repeat customers. Targeting them will get a better conversion rate. But it all starts with identifying who that ideal customer is. Let me break down some strategies you can use to gain some clarity on this so you can sell more with less effort.

Know who your ideal customer is *not* (Carl versus George).

One way to start identifying your ideal customer is to first figure out who they are not—they're often easier to spot. For example, selling a prosthetic limb to someone who has all their limbs wouldn't be the best strategy, nor would marketing leg prosthetics to people who have lost an arm. Write down examples of the types of people who would not be interested in your product.

Other less-than-ideal clients are harder to identify. Let's talk fishing. Your Uncle Carl was invited to a boy's fishing trip and needs to buy a fishing pole, but he is not the fishing store's ideal customer. You might think, "*Sure, he is! He's someone who needs a fishing pole. They sell fishing poles. BOOM! Ideal customer.*" But the *ideal* customer is not just a one-time customer. Sure, Uncle Carl is going to buy a pole for the trip, but this is the last time he is ever going to buy from that store. The fishing store's ideal customer is George, someone who loves fishing and goes every weekend he possibly can. He isn't going to buy just one pole; he is going to buy many because, believe it or not, you need different poles for different situations (although I could never figure out why he needed more than 60 poles for bass fishing alone!). And even if George didn't need more poles, he wanted them! He's also going to buy lures, fishing lines, and a fishing hat—maybe three—and a holder for all the poles to put all along one wall of the garage. So why would the fishing store focus its energy and resources to sell to 1,000 Carls when they could sell to 100 Georges?

You want to know who the "George" is among your customers. This is when you begin crafting your ideal-customer avatar (ICA).

Narrow the field; get specific.

Once you've determined who your ideal customer is not, you can start focusing on who your ideal customer is. And working on an ICA is an effective way to do so. An ICA is the avatar or persona of the *perfect* customer for your offer or product. The issue is that it requires specificity, no matter how many times you may have already gone through such a training or how much you struggle with getting specific. Many business owners fear that if they define their target customer too narrowly, they won't end up with any customers at all. But in reality, the opposite is true. The more specific you are, the easier it will be to find those customers.

When we launched GROworkspace, we were targeting Young Living Brand Partners. We knew exactly where to find them, what groups to contact, and what conventions and events to attend. If we had expanded our target audience to include everyone selling essential oils and anybody buying Young Living oils, we would have had to broaden our message and spend more time and money to try to reach all those potential customers, which would have resulted in fewer overall conversions. At the same time, the message to our target Young Living Brand Partners would have been less compelling, so our ideal-customer conversion rate would also have been lower. By focusing our money and efforts on that one community, we were able to grow a paid community of 6,000 dedicated members.

It would have been wasteful for us to focus our efforts on ads that simply targeted anyone in direct sales or anyone who sold essential oils—or to attend conferences that hosted anyone outside this one particular company. We were able to focus our efforts on building relationships with other people in this company and serving their audiences to promote their products and services. That's who our product was designed to serve. We attended conferences and set up vendor booths at events where only Young Living Brand Partners would be. We were able to quickly identify where our ideal customer was hanging out online and then put ourselves in front of them. Knowing exactly who you are serving will keep you from wasting time and money.

To start, describe your ideal customer in as much detail as possible. This is the person who will want to buy your products or services. Then, find even more targeted metrics such as personality, demographics, lifestyle, and beliefs. This gives you a way to narrow down your perfect customer—one who will buy every time you launch something new, is a pleasure to work with, and sings your praises to others. (Now that is an ideal customer!)

Targeting your ideal customer will grow your business faster and with more ease. Who do you think would be easier to sell anti-aging face cream to: a woman who is 50 or a woman who is 21? I hope you said the 50-year-old. Sure, the 21-year-old could use it to try to prevent her skin from aging, but it's going to take a whole lot less effort to sell it to someone in their 50s who's already seeing the effects of aging and looking for an anti-aging product versus trying to convince 21-year-olds who by comparison have youthful glowing skin and can't envision their skin in a future that seems light years away.

Everyone I have worked with one-on-one or as students of my programs gets scared. They say, "But my products or services can help everyone!" They are deathly afraid that if they "niche" down and target a specific person, then they won't make as many sales. But the opposite is true. When you are too broad, it has the reverse effect because when you speak to everyone, you speak to no one. By that I mean when you speak in vague terms, such that you don't "leave people out," then people don't relate or connect well and just move on. Conversely, when you get specific, when you know exactly who you are trying to attract and can describe them, then they say, "OMG, [insert your name here] is speaking right to me!" and lean in to hear more. They go to read another one of your social posts or subscribe to your email list because you have spoken to them in a way that has resonated and piqued their curiosity. This idea often appears in literature about tribal marketing, where you target customers with shared interests and beliefs.

Using direct and specific language that speaks to a specific clientele will help you draw in your ideal customer. Instead of saying generic things like, "This magic potion can help anyone sleep better. Get it while it's hot," try saying something specific like, "Baby kept you up all night? Grab this magic potion and both you and baby will sleep like an angel all night long." (On a side note, I'm pretty sure that whoever coined the term "sleep like a baby" never had one. Just saying.)

I can see why you are drawn to the first quote because anyone can use the product, and so in theory it would widen your audience, providing more opportunities to sell. But the slogan's generalizing nature prevents anyone from really connecting with it, which leads to a lack of sales. When you take the second statement, "Baby kept you up all night? Grab this magic potion and both you and baby will sleep like an angel all night long," you are now grabbing someone's attention. A mom with a baby who didn't get any sleep sees your post and feels seen. She is desperate because she is trying to function on three hours of sleep and will try anything—and poof, you just gained a customer. In fact, this message will resonate with anyone who has ever been a mom and needs sleep now. This is what getting specific about your target audience or having a niche does to your business. It puts you in your own category and makes it much more obvious that you are the one who should get their money.

I love it when I meet a business owner and they talk about a very specific person they serve, like a physical therapist who says,

"I focus on helping postpartum women with weak pelvic floors." It is so clear to me whom they can help, so any time I am at the trampoline park with my kids and a mom says, "I haven't been able to jump on one of those things since Johnny pushed his big head out!" then I know exactly whom I can recommend. If the therapist had just said, "I'm a physical therapist and I can pretty much help anyone," I wouldn't have thought of her specifically to recommend.

I have also found that niching down and picking a target audience can make things a lot easier in the beginning, but then over time, you may find that you need to broaden your niche. As discussed, we used to speak only to Young Living Brand Partners, which made it so easy to find and attract those customers. Then we started to evolve and expand our content to help others in direct sales, and then we started attracting budding entrepreneurs with our coaching services. Over time, my audience has broadened, allowing us to launch an additional brand with a new product suite of formats and payment models. Now we speak to multiple audiences about building, automating, and growing their online businesses.

Imagine a coach who teaches entrepreneurs how to use the task-management system ClickUp. At first, her target is narrow. She helps entrepreneurs use ClickUp. But then over time, as she shares more and more about all kinds of systems, she starts attracting more individuals who are using other task-management systems. Though the coach has two courses specifically for those using ClickUp, she decides to create a course to teach time-management systems for any entrepreneur with a team. Because her audience started to broaden, so did she.

The moral of the story is to not be afraid to get specific about who you want to attract. It will make finding people easier and in fact grow your business faster. It's like fishing in a barrel versus in the vast, deep ocean. Create a barrel! And if in the future you really want to broaden, do it!

Seek out those who want your product the most, not those who need it the most.

People often describe their ideal customer as the person who will have the biggest transformation with their offer, but this isn't necessarily the ideal customer either. Ideal customers are not the ones who *need* your product the most but rather the ones who really *want* what you have to offer and are ready and able to buy it.

I once had a private coaching session with Lisa, one of our most enthusiastic Build a Blissful Business students. She was in the direct-sales industry selling wellness products through an affiliate link and also wanted to attract people who would want to leverage the direct-sales business model to start their own businesses doing what she does. In the session, we were working on getting clear on her ideal customer: someone who would want to start a business in this space.

She specifically wanted to help women who are in recovery from addiction to create a life of freedom. I asked her to describe her ideal customer. She began to talk about a woman from her AA (Alcoholics Anonymous) meetings. This woman had recently joined AA and was a single mother working two jobs in order to make ends meet. As she described this woman, I could hear in her voice the passion and desire to help this woman. After she got done telling me more about her, she started to express some concerns.

When someone joins AA, they are not supposed to make any big life changes for their first year. So starting a new business would be out of the question. This was the first red flag that she wouldn't be an ideal customer because she wouldn't be in a position to accept Lisa's offer to start a business. The timing was bad for such a big life change. She also expressed concern that this woman may not have had any extra time to focus on a new business working two jobs as a single mom. This was the second red flag that she wasn't Lisa's ideal customer.

Though Lisa's potential customer might experience the biggest transformation if she built her own online business, and though Lisa desperately wanted to help people rise from rock bottom, the woman she described is in fact *not* her ideal customer because it would be incredibly challenging to build a business given her current circumstances. Remember, you want to identify your *ideal* customer, someone who you would love to work with, who will be easy to work with, and who will also get the transformation you promise with relative ease.

To help Lisa identify her true ideal customer, I asked her to think about someone she was already working with and would want to clone 100 times. She instantly thought of her best friend who was doing this business alongside her. Her friend is a self-starter, has free time to work on her business, has a desire for more in life, and is outgoing—and people are drawn to her. She doesn't need her hand held but asks questions when she needs help. Now *these* were good characteristics of an ideal customer.

Think ahead to your eventual product suite.

It's tempting to try to sell one product and look for anyone and everyone who is willing to buy it. I am begging you—please resist this temptation. You want lasting repeat customers who will buy your product or service now and then keep buying from you. In the last chapter, we talked about building a product suite. This is why you want to have a very clear idea of who your ideal dream customer is. You want to attract people who will want to buy your workshop *and* your course *and* attend your retreat *and* buy your templates. Your revenue can grow much bigger and faster if you find someone who will eventually buy all four, not just your first one. In one year alone, George signed up for a workshop on a new technology for tracking fish underwater, booked four fishing-guide sessions for his kids, bought three new poles and reels, bought another as a gift for his real-estate agent's son, and had two subscriptions to fishing magazines. If you sell or do anything related to fishing, you should clearly target George, not Carl!

Finding this kind of customer does great things for you and your business. Importantly, it helps you generate more sales with a smaller email list because your customers are buying over and over again. It also helps your cost per acquisition go down.

COST PER ACQUISITION (CPA) is a marketing metric that measures the total cost to acquire a single paying customer. It is an important way for businesses to determine whether their investment in a certain marketing channel is providing them with a maximum return on investment (ROI).

Example: If you are spending money on ads and it is costing you $30 per person to get them to buy a $15 product, then you have lost money. In this case, ads don't seem worth the investment. But if you spend $30 to acquire the ideal customer who will buy your $15 product and then go on to buy your $100 offer and join your $2,000 retreat, then that marketing strategy was effective and you had a good ROI.

Craft your ICA.

Be sure to identify all the characteristics about your ideal client and then create a profile for your ICA. You can get incredibly detailed with your ICA, down to eye color and favorite breakfast food if you want. Once you identify who this magical unicorn customer is, begin to craft your messaging around this ICA with the goal of attracting 100 such potential customers.

Having gained some clarity regarding your ideal customer, now identify the main and most important characteristics of this person by considering the following questions in a way that points to how your offer can personally help them.

- What are their problems?
- What keeps them up at night?
- What are the solutions they are looking for?
- What are their desires?

Identify and eliminate their limiting beliefs.

With your ICA in mind, this is the time to think about the limiting beliefs of your ideal client, beliefs that you need them to break. This will affect how you craft your messages to market your offer. For example, if you help someone lose weight, a limiting belief might be that you can't lose weight without going on a strict diet. If you want to teach people how to lose weight while still eating cookies, it is incredibly important that your ideal customer believes that you can in fact lose weight while still eating cookies.

Limiting beliefs limit sales, so it's important to identify your target customer's limiting beliefs. By identifying the most common limiting beliefs, you can work to break them and decrease barriers to purchasing your offer. Our *Build a Blissful Business* training goes into this in depth not only to help you identify limiting beliefs but also then learn how to break them to increase sales and client results.

Take some time to think about who your ideal customer is. I have an in-depth process my clients go through to sort this out, but you can start by writing down your ideal-customer profile. Make sure you are clear on their lifestyle and interests, the limiting beliefs holding them back from buying, and solutions they are open to explore. Knowing and understanding them like they are your best friends will help you speak in a way that connects, helps them feel seen and heard, and draws them in for more so they get on your email list and buy.

PART II

WORKING EFFICIENTLY IN YOUR BUSINESS THROUGH SYSTEMS, AUTOMATION, AND PROCESSES

CHAPTER 6

CREATE A SALES FUNNEL TO TRANSFORM TRAFFIC TO LEADS AND THEN TO CUSTOMERS

To begin to turn your offer into a blissful business, you first need a strategic sales funnel to make it rain gold! The goal is to develop a manageable and automated system to save you time on a day-to-day basis, giving you more bandwidth to focus on the things that matter to you most while generating a stupid amount of revenue. If it's set up correctly and automated, it should literally sell for you while you sleep because your traffic is seamlessly turning into leads who are then turning into customers.

What is a sales funnel?

A sales funnel is the path you create to lead your audience to buy your offer. Imagine a funnel that you would use to pour water from a bucket into a small bottle. The water poured into the funnel has a clear and direct path to exactly where you want it to go. The purpose of the funnel is to eventually get all the water through the funnel without spilling. Similarly, your sales funnel is wide at the top because you start with all the people who are aware of your product. Although only a small percentage will make their way to the bottom to become customers, your funnel will provide a clear and direct path to that end. You will first generate traffic, then turn your traffic into leads, funnel people through your nurture and sales sequence, and finally move them on to become your customers.

The top of your funnel represents your total *traffic*. You will attract traffic from various places: YouTube, social media, guest speaking, local meetups. Then you will funnel those you attract into your *lead-generation* step. This is the step where you hope to turn interest in your offer into an actionable desire by presenting a free gift (challenge, workshop, checklist, template) in exchange for the potential customer's email. Then you will move potential customers into the *nurture and sales sequence*, which will warm them up, highlight the problem that attracts them to your offer, and present your offer as the solution to that problem. This is commonly done through emails or text messages. If they *purchase*, they will have successfully gone through your funnel and turned into a customer.

Awareness Phase: Generate traffic to build awareness.
You need traffic at the top of your funnel. In other words, potential customers need to become aware of your brand. It may seem obvious, but **if they don't know you exist, they can't buy from you**. To build awareness, you can use free, valuable, short- or long-form content such as a blog, podcast, YouTube video, or social-media post, just to name a few. The goal is to provide ample opportunity for people to find you online so they become aware of the value you offer them.

There are many places you can find people who are interested in what you have to offer: local businesses, communities, meetup groups, parents at your child's school or on sports teams, online communities, masterminds, Facebook groups, LinkedIn. YouTube and guest speaking for other people's audiences are two of my preferred ways to find people or have people find me. YouTube is particularly suited for this task because once you create the video content, it lives there forever. As more people search for solutions to their problems, YouTube is sending them to your video, allowing you to continue to attract people who will want what you have to offer. Guest speaking in groups or on podcasts is another popular method because you are placing yourself in front of an audience that someone else has already built. If you are strategic about seeking out someone with an audience of people filled with your ideal customers, you can get more and faster exposure and traffic to your website and freebie.

To accomplish this kind of awareness quickly, collaborate. I learned this as I was sitting at a pool, laid back in the lounge chair watching the kids dive for rubber rings. My phone started blowing up with Facebook notifications telling me 500 people were trying to join a recent group I'd created. Every hour, there were another 1,000 people to accept. I took screenshots and sent them to my sister with excitement! How was this happening? It was in that moment that I realized the power of collaboration and cross-promotion.

I had set up a Facebook group with the intention of hosting a week-long event where a variety of specialists, including a chiropractor, teacher, massage therapist, doula, and nurse, would come in and teach about how they were using essential oils personally and professionally to grow oils businesses alongside their regular businesses. At the time, I was really a nobody in the Young Living community, but I had a vision for a resource that would and could only be created through a collaborative effort. The only option I really had was to cold message people that I wanted to participate and ask if they would be open to speaking.

The smartest thing I could've ever done was first reach out to Jim Bob Haggerton, a popular chiropractor in the Young Living community who everybody knew and loved. "Fortune is for the bold," they say. Well, when he said yes, 99 percent of the other people I approached did the same. You better believe I included that piece of information when I reached out to everyone else. "Jim Bob said yes! Would you speak too?" By the time the event started just four weeks later, the group had over 45,000 essential-oil enthusiasts eager to learn!

I will be forever grateful to the amazing group that participated in my first-ever collaborative virtual event in the Essential Oils for Professionals Facebook group. I had NO idea what I was doing! It was before I had any online business outside direct sales—no email swipe copy for them to share, no sales funnel to get people to sign up and join my email list. The truth is, at that time, I wasn't trying to sell anything to people in the group. I just wanted the resources to offer to my community as a tool and figured, "Why not open it up to everyone else for free?" That ended up being the true catalyst for building my audience for a future business. Massive virtual events aren't the only way to grow your traffic. Leverage your network to get on podcasts or speak in communities. Small, steady growth can also win the race.

PRO TIP

Relationships take time, so start building them now, as it can be incredibly impactful for your business. Some of the best collaborations happen between you and the people you have a relationship with, but every now and again, it doesn't hurt to ask someone you don't know. They might just surprise you with a YES!—and if not, just keep moving forward.

Interest Phase: Increase interest to generate leads for your email list.

In the Lead-Generation Phase, or as I like to call it, the Interest Phase, you build a way to get someone's contact information, especially their email address, directly into your funnel that already has traffic. A great way to do this is to offer a free gift. This step is invaluable in moving potential customers along in their journey with you.

Building and leveraging an email list is going to be the most effective way to get people familiar with you, your content, and your offers on a regular basis. You might think that people don't open emails anymore or that email is dead when it comes to the marketing world. Email has been around for a long time, and it is still highly effective. When you fill your email list with people excited about what you have to offer, you can generate a lot of revenue simply through emails. **I've sent out a single email blast and generated $39,000 in sales in one day.**

Even though growing your email list is critical to increase sales, with the right strategies, you can generate significant interest and income with even just a small list. My friend Emily, who teaches women how to become virtual assistants and work from

SELL WHILE YOU SLEEP

home, launched her first digital course to a list of 60 people—a list she grew over about four months. Twenty of them purchased her course, and she made over $2,000 during her first launch. Over the next three years, she continued to grow her email list and sell her offers. In her latest launch, she leveraged her email list of 5,000 engaged people and generated over $136,000 in revenue in just one week.

PRO TIP

Though Emily started selling only after her list of people was up to 60, you can start selling your offer as soon as it's ready and not wait until you have built up your email list, as waiting will stall your potential to bring in sales now. Leverage the connections in your circle that might be your ideal customers while you build your email list, reaching out to them and sharing how your offer can help them. This will help you get your feet wet and help you bring in income right away while you set up your funnel and build your email list to convert customers on autopilot. Over time, your list and revenues will grow. Be patient yet consistent and leverage what I teach you here to do it in the most effective and efficient way possible.

Regardless of where you are building an audience, whether from YouTube, Instagram, LinkedIn, TikTok, or elsewhere, it's imperative you drive traffic from those platforms to your email list because it allows you to control the messaging and ensures you land right in front of them instead of relying on ever-changing algorithms on such platforms as Instagram or Facebook that may or may not put your content in front of your ideal customer.

To put things into perspective, a 5 percent reach is a "good" reach rate on Instagram, according to Hootsuite, a popular third-party site that allows users to schedule posts to Instagram. This means that when you post your short-form content on a platform such as Instagram, it's likely only around 5 percent of those following your page will see your content. Of course, there is a decent likelihood that non-followers might see your content, but they may not be your ideal customers and there is no guarantee they will see any future messages.

According to the popular email marketing platform Constant Contact, email marketing has an 89.9 percent average send rate and a 34.46 percent average open rate across all industries, which means your email is landing in about 90 percent of the inboxes from your email list and 34 percent of the people on your email list will read your message.[2] Though your social-media following could be much larger than your email list, I will argue that your social-media audience could be a wide range of not-so-ideal customers, whereas your email list, if you are drawing them in correctly, is going to be a list of much more serious customers because of the extra effort they have exerted to get on your email list; they will have had to enter their email address rather than just hit the follow button. Furthermore, according to Forbes, email marketing has a 4,500 percent ROI. That means if you spend one dollar, you could receive 45 dollars.[3]

To show that I practice what I preach, I can tell you that for our 2023 spring launch of Build a Blissful Business, I used all avenues of promotion *except* social media. During the three-week promotional time, I posted to social media fewer than five times. Meanwhile, I grew my email list by 1,200 contacts by leveraging affiliates and ended with a $115,000 launch and $86,000 in profit.

Social media took a backseat in promotion, and to this day, I still make most of my sales through email marketing. The value is high, and email marketing has been a critical part of our long-term growth and sales strategy. This is also where a large part of automation takes place.

Though social media can be used effectively to build your email list, it's also time consuming—not to mention that you can lose all your content and followers if it gets hacked, which I found out the hard way. But it works well for some. For example, my friend Holly leverages Instagram to grow her following, but she directs people to join her email list almost instantly with her free offer, turning her followers into email subscribers she can take through her funnel.

Because it is free, I do recommend leveraging social media to drive traffic to your website and increase your email list. However, that is just one of many different ways you can grow your business—and the best part is you get to decide what is best for you. Regardless of what method you use, you will have to put in the effort to get in front of people. And if you don't, your customers will find someone else to follow.

PRO TIP

Talk about your free offering in every blog, podcast, and YouTube video. Put the link to your freebie on your menu bar on your website, in your email signature, on your social media bios, and anywhere else people find you. If you don't talk about it, share it, and make it easy for people to get to, they won't get on your email list, which you need to move them down through your funnel.

Once people in your funnel trade their email for your free gift or training, your email-marketing platform will send them the automated email you previously set up with the gift inside—no action needed on your part. The gift might be a guide, workshop, training, or template—the gift itself is not as important as the fact that you got a new lead further down into your funnel. It's important that this freebie helps them get a quick win to get them excited and hence prepared to pay for your main offer. Think of your freebie as a free sample of dessert given out at your local supermarket—it leaves you wanting more! It's an easy-to-consume piece of content that gets them hooked for the next phase—a gateway with nothing but positive consequences.

After the free-gift email, you will send a few more automated emails over the ensuing week or two to help deepen the recipients' desire for your offer. You can use a variety of strategies, from product or service information to storytelling, case studies, or testimonials.

Desire Phase: Nurture your email list and build desire.
This is a series of content, most commonly shared through automated emails, that you use to continue to build trust with your potential customers once they've joined your email list. Through a series of emails, you will highlight the problem they are having and present your offer as the solution to that problem. This nurture sequence will bring them to the third phase: the Desire Phase. The goal in this phase is to get potential customers primed and ready so they are already wishing they had your offer before you ever offer it to them. Simply put, they desire what you have to offer!

Purchase Phase: Turn leads into customers.

When done right, your audience can move quickly from the Desire Phase into the Purchase Phase and pay for a monetized offer. If you focus on building traffic, generating more leads, and nurturing your potential customers, like we just talked about, then more of your traffic will move all the way through your funnel from awareness to interest to desire to purchase. You will now have customers—YOUR customers!

Content

Now that you are aware of the way your funnel works, let's take a closer look at the ways you can use content to create traffic and awareness, to increase interest through a freebie, and to nurture your customers to create connection with and a loyal following of customers.

Content is any piece of information you create and share: graphics or copy for social media, blogs, webinars, PDFs, slide decks, podcast episodes, videos. And like it or not, creating content is absolutely critical to your success. You want to develop content to bring people's problems to light, break limiting beliefs that might hold them back from purchasing, and share value so they want to keep coming back for more.

There are important pieces of content to grow your audience in the Awareness and Interest Phases of your sales funnel that lead them to the Desire and Purchase Phases. Both your short- and long-form content offers an opportunity for others to get to know you. As you share stories, case studies, and tips, they learn about you and how you can help them, and they start to get a sense of whether they want to move closer into your circle by paying for your help. This content should also drive traffic to your free offer to build the email list that you can use to deliver more content to increase desire for your offer. Let's dive in to learn more about these different forms of content.

Short-Form Content

Short-form content includes snippets of information to introduce a concept or give a quick tip to get people intrigued and excited to learn more. Short-form content may be text, a photo, or video. Oftentimes, your short-form content can direct customers directly to your free offer in exchange for providing their email address, or it can direct them to long-form content where they can get more information. If social-media platforms are going to be your main platform on which to build your audience, try to create at least three pieces of short-form content a week, creating new content to share daily. If social media is not your jam, then you will need to focus your efforts elsewhere to get in front of your ideal customers: collaboration, attending local meetups, leaving your information at businesses, or using paid ads, just to name a few.

Types of Short-Form Content

Product teasers: This content gives only a little information about your product, with more information to be shared later, and can be used in the release of a new product or offer. The purpose is to grab attention and get people curious. If you are releasing a new course in collaboration with a friend, you can tease the course with information about you and your partner and why you are the best duo to help them. If you are releasing a new product line, you can share that something big is coming that will change the way your ideal customer does something.

Behind the scenes (BTS): BTS content shows just that: behind the scenes of your business, life, or product. If you make jewelry, you could film the process of you creating a specific piece. Speed up the video using a free mobile app such as InShot and show an hour-long process to create in under 10 seconds. People generally find these videos to be highly entertaining. If you are a mom selling her homeschool courses, you could create a short video of you creating lesson plans. To help make sure the videos are entertaining to viewers, use a BTS as an eye-catching background and overlay valuable information on-screen. This can be done right inside the Instagram app or using mobile apps such as InShot. Your BTS content can share the most honest snapshots of what it's really like outside a perfect social-media feed. It helps people connect with you as it makes you more relatable because you are sharing the true, honest work that goes into what you do.

Educational content: Provide educational information to build awareness about what you do. You can build awareness around your ICA's problem—even just helping them see that they have a problem. For example, since Claire and I help people build their websites and funnels, we might create a piece of content demonstrating how certain brand colors and fonts might be detrimental to sales.

You can also create educational content that highlights the benefits of your product or provides a solution to your problems. An esthetician might share how microblading (tattooing on eyebrows) can create a natural, full eyebrow appearance that lasts three to five years, thereby eliminating the need to pencil in your eyebrows every day. Someone selling toxin-free products could share the harmful effects that your toxin-filled products are causing on your health and positioning their products as the safe solution.

Where do you want to share your short-form content?
Think about where your customers spend their time online. If you aren't sure, look at your competitors. Where are they sharing their content? Take a poll of your existing audience to find out where they prefer to spend their time.

Here is a list of popular social-media platforms to consider for your business:

Facebook: The OG of social-media platforms. It's the largest, with three billion monthly users. Great for sharing almost any kind of content: pictures, videos, articles, GIFs. It's also a great platform to host a community inside its Groups feature.

Instagram: A visual sharing platform where you can share photos and short videos and go live for your audience.

Threads: An Instagram brand designed to be a competitor to X (formally Twitter). You must have an Instagram account in order to have a Threads account.

TikTok: Created and owned by a Chinese company, it's one of the most popular and fastest-growing apps in the world. Used for short-form video sharing.

Snapchat: Focuses on short videos shared between friends, with 69 percent of teens acknowledging that they are on the platform. If you are targeting teens, this is a great place to be.

LinkedIn: A professional networking platform to share content and build your personal brand.

Substack: Popular for writers as a free press platform to share your articles.

YouTube: Video-based platform that's good for both short- and long-form videos. Solution-based searching platform that makes it easier for your ideal customers to find your content.

Pinterest: Used for inspiration and discovering new products and ideas. A great feature is the ability to share "Pins," which are photos (short-form content) that direct traffic to blogs, product pages, and websites (long-form content).

X (formerly Twitter): Used for real-time information. Popular for news, politics, sports, entertainment, and more. It has also turned into an alternative customer-service channel for businesses.

Tumblr: Customizable platform used for microblogging. Text, photos, videos, GIFs, audio clips, and links can also be shared on this platform.

Discord: An app for gamers to connect with communities and chat in real time.

Twitch: A live-streaming app for gamers and e-sports communities.

Meetup: A platform used to meet new people, get out of your comfort zone, and explore passions together. If your business involves local services and gatherings, this app can be useful.

Other apps worth noting on which to list your business (not really for sharing short-from content):

PublicSquare: Largest network of American patriot-owned businesses. A great place for freedom-loving customers to find your freedom-loving business.

Communication Apps to include on your website:

WhatsApp: Less of a community app and used more for people to communicate with your business. Owned by Meta (Facebook).

WeChat: Similar to WhatsApp but owned by a Chinese company. It has turned into an all-in-one place for messaging, shopping, paying bills, transferring money, and more.

You don't need to be everywhere at the same time. Though you'll want to focus on the place where you will find your ideal customers, if social media overwhelms you, pick one platform you are most comfortable with and start there.

Long-Form Content

Long-form content is pieces of content that have over 1,000 words, such as blog posts, five- to ten-minute YouTube videos, podcasts, or newsletters. But don't get fooled by the word "long"—it doesn't need to be an hour or 3,000 words. Long-form content allows you to go deeper and share more than the snippets found in short-form content. If you are strictly relying on organic (unpaid) traffic, then I highly recommend creating at least one piece of long-form content to share weekly. This allows you to continue to maximize your reach. Different people and businesses can thrive better with different types of long-form content. See what type resonates with you and then set a plan to release at least one long-form piece of content a month, building to release one a week.

Types of Long-Form Content

Blog: If you love to write and are deathly afraid to put yourself in front of the camera, then a blog can be a great way to provide valuable information and teach your audience. The great thing about a blog is that when you're using keywords that your target audience uses, your blog post has a better chance of popping up as a suggested article for them to read because it has good SEO (search-engine optimization), meaning that the search engines (Google, Yahoo!, DuckDuckGo, Bing) are looking for relevant articles that match user searches. In your blog, send your reader to grab your freebie and get them on your email list. A blog can be especially valuable for small and midsize businesses with a global reach: software businesses, product-based businesses, even businesses with high-ticket offers. You can use a blog to get exposure sharing about your topic of expertise.

> **EXAMPLE**: A CPA who sells a bookkeeping course could create a blog post called Three Tips to Better Bookkeeping for Your Small Business. The blog shares three tips about bookkeeping and at the end instructs the reader to download a FREE bookkeeping spreadsheet to help them implement the tips. Using the spreadsheet gives them a quick win and invests them in his services. Exchanging their email for the free spreadsheet puts the reader into the CPA's funnel, where he can then deepen the user's desire and pitch his course Bookkeeping for Small Businesses.

If writing is not your forte, then consider another option.

Podcasts: If speaking is what you are most comfortable with, consider starting a podcast. Podcasts can range from five minutes to three+ hours. You can keep it as simple as recording yourself speaking through your phone and uploading the audio onto a podcast platform. There are many podcast platforms that are free, such as Anchor, Podbean, and Buzzsprout. Done is better than perfect, so start simple, and if you want, add music or a special introduction to start your podcast; you can always start incorporating it later. I cringe whenever anyone tells me they went back and listened to my first podcast episode, as it wasn't my best work, but we all must start somewhere—and with more practice, you are sure to improve!

In terms of the length of your podcast, think about your audience and what time they can afford to spend. I noticed that the downloads greatly increased when my episodes changed from 45 to 60 minutes to under 20 minutes. My audience is busy, and shorter episodes make it easier to consume. Plus, it is easier for me to produce more episodes when they are shorter, so it is a win-win. However, your topic may require long podcasts, and your audience may love listening. At the end of the day, determine what your audience wants, couple it with what works for you, and create.

Having a podcast also makes it easier to get on other people's podcasts because you can do a podcast swap. You bring someone on to your podcast and then they will bring you onto theirs. If guest speaking on other podcasts is a method you want to leverage for audience exposure and you feel it would be a good method of delivering your content, I highly recommend starting your own podcast.

If your teaching requires visuals, like an artist who teaches watercolor painting, then podcasting may not be the best option. You may prefer YouTube videos for your visual lessons and supplement them with topics suitable for podcasts such as art theory, ways to get inspired, time management, or how to sell your art. You could interview various artists to hear more about their stories and where their inspiration comes from.

YouTube videos: No one initially thinks of YouTube as a search engine, but it is. People go to YouTube and type in something they are looking for into the search bar: "how to sew a cross-stitch," "ab exercises for postpartum moms," "how to create a lead magnet on Canva." YouTube searches its database and tries to give users the most relevant videos. This is why I love this platform for long-form content. The people who find your video are literally looking for the solutions you have to offer. Another reason I love it is because over time, your views will grow, unlike social media, where it's less likely for people to find your old posts.

PRO TIP

Think about what your ideal customer is searching for on YouTube, come up with a title that includes those key words, and then create your video around that title.

Start with short videos if time is of the essence. Again, you don't need any fancy production—stop using that as an excuse. As your business grows, you can decide whether having fancy production on your videos would help you attract and sell more, but for now, keep it simple. Turn on your computer, go to a video-recording app (I use QuickTime because it's already built into my

MacBook), and hit record. Be sure to provide your viewer with the URL to go to and get their free gift, leave the link in the video description, and remind them to subscribe to your channel before they exit the video.

Regardless of where you are sharing long-form content, you always want to drive traffic to your free gift to grow your email list. Remember to share *why* people will find your free gift valuable and provide simple and clear instructions on how to get it.

Once you pick your preferred method of delivering long-form content, consider repurposing your content to maximize your reach. You can take the content from your podcast episode and turn it into a YouTube video or a blog post in seconds by leveraging artificial intelligence (AI) such as ChatGPT. Then you'll have a blog, podcast, and YouTube video all with the same information.

Content for Your Free Gift/Offer

Your free gift or offer can be anything from a downloadable checklist to a prerecorded or live workshop to a minicourse to a 15-minute consultation. Of course, in order to save time and have the ability to scale your business, I highly recommend using giveaways that can be accessed without one-on-one attention. A hundred thousand people can download a checklist every week, but you can only take so many 15-minute one-on-one consultation calls. Keep this in mind when deciding on your freebie.

When you are trying to decide on your free offer, consider where your ideal client would find value and what a perfect first step to get them excited for your paid offer would be. Like the CPA from before, a free bookkeeping spreadsheet to help someone keep track of and organize their business expenses is the perfect first step to help someone who will ultimately be looking for a more robust course about small-business bookkeeping.

Types of Free-Gift/Offer Content

Templates, checklists, or guides: People love templates, checklists, and guides even more than they do training videos. They want anything to help them stay organized and speed up their processes. (Hello! It's why you bought this book!) Society has groomed us to want instant information and fast results. A checklist, PDF guide, worksheet, or template all help your community get what they need faster and in a more organized way.

Trainings or masterclasses: If you need to provide more in-depth information, this could be a good option. A fitness instructor could offer a 15-minute six-pack-abs training video as her free offer. Though it's more typical to see a one- to two-hour masterclass pitch an offer in the range of $300 to $2,000, a mini masterclass can be successful at a variety of price points and offer types.

Recipe guides or e-books: These digital offers are typically in the form of a PDF. Don't let the word "book" scare you. An e-book could be as little as 10 pages. My friend Holly Hillyer sells nutrition plans through her direct-sales company, BODi, and has been able to increase her sales by 25 percent using an automated email funnel. She is crushing it with her Favorite Dessert Recipe Book freebie. She markets the free recipe book as her favorite desserts that she ate while losing 47 pounds postpartum. People are eating it up like crazy! (Pun intended!) By conveying that she'd lost weight eating these desserts, she is attracting people who want to lose weight while still eating what they love. Selling nutrition plans at the end of the funnel is an easy sell for the women she is attracting through her strategic marketing: women wanting to lose weight without going on a strict diet.

Discount codes: Discount codes are popular for product- or service-based businesses. It seems like every site I go to has a pop-up that says, "Unlock 10% off your first order now!" To get the code for 10 percent off, you must subscribe to their email list. Once you're subscribed, they send you an automated email with a code for the 10 percent off.

Newsletters or waitlists: You can also direct people to sign up for your email list so they can receive a regular newsletter or join a wait list for your paid offer. But remember: people covet their emails. They must really want what you have to be willing to trade their email address. A "join my newsletter" message isn't very impactful. Instead, try something like this: "Sign up for our exclusive monthly newsletter to get my best tips to grow your business."

If you are leveraging a wait list to grow your email list, what will they get if they join your wait list? You could, for example, give them access to an exclusive bonus for when they later buy your offer. Or you might give them a discount or first dibs on joining something that only has limited space: "Join the wait list and get early-bird access before the doors are officially open! Only 10 spaces available."

Though there are a variety of types of free offers, you only need one to start. So be strategic about what you are picking so it's highly effective.

As for me, it was 2017 and I was teaching yoga classes at a local yoga studio when one day I started chatting with an amazing guy who was cleaning the yoga studio in exchange for free yoga classes. I learned that his day job was marketing for small businesses. I shared with him my new business venture and told him I had access to a Facebook group of 45,000 people but no email list to promote our paid membership. He agreed to an hour-long consultation with Claire and me during which he shared his strategy of leveraging a downloadable free gift to grow an email list.

The key here was to figure out what we could offer that would attract our ideal customer from the Facebook group to sign up for our email list so we could pitch them our paid offer through a strategically automated series of emails. We were specifically seeking out Young Living Brand Partners interested in building an essential-oils business, so we decided to offer 90 Days of Income-Producing Activities Checklist for Young Living Brand Partners. This would certainly only appeal to those building a business with Young Living and not to people who were strictly product users.

Within two weeks of promoting the free checklist into the Facebook group, we had over 3,000 people signed up for our email list. People were almost instantly joining the paid membership, and after four months, we had successfully taken 8,000 people through our funnel and 4,000 of them turned into purchasers. Though these numbers are not typical, they are possible when you have a large audience or drive a massive amount of traffic to your freebie. This was when I realized that the unimaginable can happen when you combine a strategic, automated funnel, clarity about your ideal customer, and the right freebie with the right messaging to promote and sell your main offer in your email-marketing sequence.

CHAPTER 7

AUTOMATE YOUR FUNNEL

We talked in chapter 6 about creating your funnel. Now you want to automate your funnel so you can make money while you sleep. If you truly want a blissful business that allows you to work less and earn more, **embracing automation is key**. It is your secret weapon to build sales efficiently. Using automation to your advantage will put you even closer to your dream life. Automation frees up your time and allows you to scale into a seven-figure-plus business while you're sipping piña coladas on the beach in Bermuda. Follow the chart on the next page to see the natural flow of your funnel and how every step can be automated.

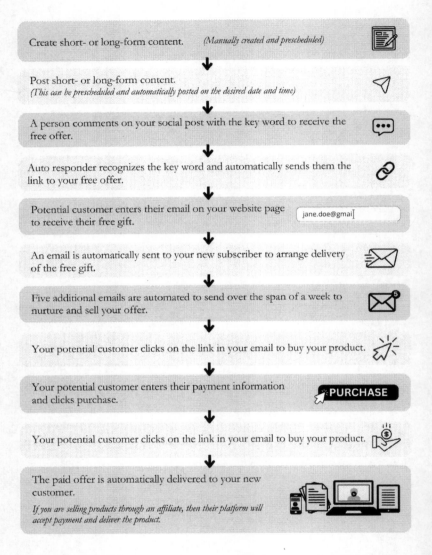

Create short- or long-form content. *(Manually created and prescheduled)*

Post short- or long-form content.
(This can be prescheduled and automatically posted on the desired date and time)

A person comments on your social post with the key word to receive the free offer.

Auto responder recognizes the key word and automatically sends them the link to your free offer.

Potential customer enters their email on your website page to receive their free gift.

An email is automatically sent to your new subscriber to arrange delivery of the free gift.

Five additional emails are automated to send over the span of a week to nurture and sell your offer.

Your potential customer clicks on the link in your email to buy your product.

Your potential customer enters their payment information and clicks purchase.

Your potential customer clicks on the link in your email to buy your product.

The paid offer is automatically delivered to your new customer.
If you are selling products through an affiliate, then their platform will accept payment and deliver the product.

In order to get your funnel automated, you will need software to connect your content and accomplish the automations.

What You Will Need

Opt-In Landing Page

First, to automate your funnel to make your life incredibly simple, you will need a website opt-in landing page. Let's break this down a bit. First, a landing page is a web page someone lands on after executing a search. The purpose of the landing page will determine what *type* of landing page you create. A landing page that collects emails is called an "opt-in" page. One that highlights your offer is called a "sales" page. One you share after someone purchases is called a "thank you" page. The main page of your website is the "home" page. A page that shares more about you or your company is often referred to as an "about" page. Though you will want to leverage all these types of landing pages for your business, you should start with an "opt-in" landing page to market your free-gift offer and collect email addresses. We build our landing pages on Kajabi.

CRM System

Because you are going to collect email addresses, you will need an email system, often referred to as a CRM (customer-relationship management) system. A CRM system allows you to collect names and email addresses and send automated emails, which, as we talked about in the previous chapter, is incredibly important to conserve your time and energy. This type of system also allows you to email all your contacts at once or segment your list into groups to only email a portion of your list at a given time. For example, you could segment your list by demographics, personality type, or actions they have taken previously.

Using a CRM system is much more efficient than operating your email through Gmail or Outlook. Imagine if you had an email list of 100 people and you decide to run a sale, you can create an email to promote that sale and then send it to all of them at once. Your funnel will require several emails to be sent over a short amount of time, which will be easily automated with your CRM system. We use the CRM system offered inside Kajabi.

Checkout Page

Though a sales page is desirable to showcase your offer, break limiting beliefs, highlight the benefits of your offer, list payment options, give guarantees, and post frequently asked questions, you will still need a checkout page where you can highlight what is included in your offer, link your terms of purchase, and accept payments. We use Kajabi checkout pages. Another popular checkout-page platform is ThriveCart.

Payment Processor

You will want to leverage a payment system such as Stripe, PayPal, or Kajabi Payments to collect payments for your offers. All payment systems take a small fee for processing payments—there is no way around it. We use Kajabi Payments as it allows us to accept any major credit card, Google Pay, PayPal, and AfterPay. AfterPay is a company that allows you to offer payment plans, but instead of you overseeing collection of each payment, AfterPay will pay you the full price of your offer up front, less their fees, and then will be responsible for collecting all the payments and handling any missed payments.

Course-Hosting Software

Depending on the type of offer you are selling, you may need software to host your offer. If you are creating and selling a digital course, you will want course-hosting software. If your offer is to join a community, then you will want software that is designed for communities. We use (you guessed it!) Kajabi for our workshops, courses, group programs, and community.

All-in-One Platform

You can certainly find software specific to each part of the funnel and each offer, but I highly recommend leveraging an all-in-one software platform so you do not have to integrate multiple platforms together to have the automation run smoothly.

We started with and continue to use an all-in-one platform called Kajabi. By creating an account with Kajabi, we can host our website, landing pages, CRM system, courses, communities, blogs, payments, and affiliate program and other features all in one place, which means we don't have to integrate multiple platforms to have everything we need to run our business.

Advantages of an All-in-One Platform

An all-in-one platform allows all your client and business information to be housed in one location, making it extremely efficient when the need arises to search for any specific information. Whether you need to look up what offers someone has purchased, what emails have been sent, analytics on landing pages, or payments, you have one login, with all the information in one place.

All-in-one platforms make automation run even more seamlessly. This means you use one company to host your email list, your offers, and payment processing. All three will communicate with each other to trigger automations. If you don't have an all-in-one platform with all three of these, it will be difficult to figure out how to integrate everything to be able to automate follow-up emails after purchases have been made. Things can misfire, and you might need to pay for third-party software to get the communication you need.

There was a brief period when we were using Kajabi to host our course, ThriveCart to take payments at checkout, and Active-Campaign to send emails. After several people emailed us to let us know they didn't get automatic access to the offer, we realized that our integration wasn't working properly. We had several other incidents when the automations weren't working because of multi-platform integration, which cost us money and created unhappy customers, so we went back to using only Kajabi to keep everything simple and effective.

Though some might think these all-in-one platforms are more expensive than using a free account on WordPress to build a website and then piecing the other software together, by the time you add up all the software platforms you need to get the job done, you often find yourself paying more than you would for an all-in-one platform such as Kajabi and then have to manage multiple subscriptions and logins.

Disadvantages of an All-in-One Platform

The main disadvantage of all-in-one platforms is that when, as the saying goes, you are a jack of all trades, you are a master of none. There are other software systems that can do a lot more because it is their sole focus. For example, ActiveCampaign, a type of CRM software, will have more features that can customize the way emails are sent or triggered. Affiliate software such as ThriveCart will have more analytics regarding your affiliates' statistics for better tracking. Nevertheless, sometimes the simplicity of an all-in-one is much better to manage and use, especially when you are just getting started. Though we are more seasoned, we still use Kajabi because, so far, every time we have ventured outside of Kajabi and used other platforms that we thought might be better, we have found ourselves coming back to Kajabi for everything.

> ## PRO TIP
>
> When you are looking into all-in-one software, pay attention to and compare features, such as how many contacts you can have before needing to upgrade or how many emails you are able to send and whether they will take a percentage of your sales. All payment-processing services such as Stripe and PayPal take a fee per transaction, but not all website/course-hosting platforms do. Some course-hosting platforms, such as our favorite Kajabi, charge a flat fee and otherwise let you keep 100 percent of the income from your sales. I highly encourage you to find one that takes *no* fees based on your success and just charges a flat fee. These are all things to pay attention to so you can keep a good handle on your expenses. Try to anticipate what features you will need long term and pick a platform that you can grow into versus having to change platforms once you grow—it can be time consuming and expensive to move all your content from one platform to the next.

Automation to Drive Traffic to Your Free Gift and Offer

Just because you build it doesn't mean they will come. Once your funnel is set up, you need to drive traffic to your free gift. This is the 20 percent of your business you want to focus on 80 percent of the time. You can use the organic advertising methods we have discussed in this chapter, or you can use paid advertising.

Organic Advertising

Organic advertising is when you drive traffic to your content and offers for free. This can be accomplished in a variety of ways. People can be driven to your content and feed into the traffic in your funnel through organic (free) advertising you do by creating your website or YouTube videos that people find on their own by searching on the internet. People may organically see your social-media posts due to the platform's algorithms alone, hear you speak on a podcast, see an affiliate post about your content, or see a flyer in a local business, all of which are popular ways to drive organic traffic to your freebie or other content. Though it feels affordable, especially when starting your business, it does cost you time.

Paid Advertising

You can also pay for advertising to send increased traffic into your funnel. You could pay to run ads on Google, YouTube, Facebook, Instagram, or Pinterest—or even your local newspaper or radio. You could pay to be a sponsor of an event like a virtual summit or run an advertisement on someone else's podcast. You could pay to have a vendor booth. There are many ways to invest your marketing dollars to get more eyes on your content about your freebies and monetized offers. Paid advertising can be a great option to drive a large amount of traffic to your content with very little effort on your part. You will want to make sure that when you pay for traffic that you measure the ROI so you can determine whether you got your money's worth.

Loving Your Automated Funnel

Having an automated funnel can completely change your business and how you spend your time daily. Without having to worry about each email, post, and payment, you can spend more time identifying additional offers, creating new content, and working on the strategic plan of your business. Who wouldn't love more time to do things like that? That's exactly why you will love your automated funnel—because it gives you back one of your most valuable gifts: your time.

Take Jennifer, one of our Build a Blissful Business students. She was exhausted, feeling like she was consumed with sending texts and emails to prospects and customers all day long. She didn't have any time for the things she really wanted to do, such as host in-person events, connect with people on a deeper level, and create resources her community had requested. She joined our program wanting to automate her Young Living direct-sales business. She used our pre-built Canva templates to create her free gift and our copywriting templates to write her email-marketing sequence as well as her "home," "about," and "contact" website pages. She also automated her entire onboarding process for her new customers to ensure they were set up for success from the get-go using our training and templates.

Though she was provided with the predesigned website-page templates for AttractWell (the all-in-one software she decided to use) inside Build a Blissful Business, she opted to hire our team to design her website in order to get it done even faster. Once it was all set up, she couldn't stop raving about how much time she had gained back on a day-to-day basis with the systems and automations in place and how well supported her community was without her needing to spend unneeded extra time with each person individually.

Advanced Strategy to Make Your Funnel More Profitable

You will make your funnel more profitable by leveraging upsells and downsells to increase your revenue. Upsells are when a person buys something from you and you offer something additional to their order. A downsell is an offer that you make at a lower price when someone has not purchased your original offer. This could be offered immediately or it could be offered weeks later as an alternative option.

Playing and experimenting with different offers, upsells, and downsells can be fun and enlightening for your business. It's also an incredible revenue generator. As an example, I once had an idea for an offer where I brought in experts to train my community on topics that are not my area of expertise, such as taxes, bookkeeping, media, and more. It's called Access to the Experts. I offered the first training to my email list for $35, but I didn't get nearly as many sales as I had hoped, so I thought about what I really wanted out of this offer. What I wanted even more than sales was live attendance. I decided to shift my strategy and email my entire list with a link to attend live for free. But in addition to getting people to attend live, I still wanted to leverage this to bring in revenue. I thought outside the box and gave myself permission to play and experiment. I told myself not to get too attached to the revenue outcome and to instead use this as an opportunity to learn.

After people entered their name and email to get the link to attend live for free, I redirected them to a website landing page that offered an upsell. If they wanted to ask our guest expert a question after the training and get the replay emailed to them, they would pay $35. There were two buttons on the landing page. One read "Yes, I want to upgrade my ticket" and the other "No thanks, I'll just attend live." When they clicked the button that said "yes," they were directed to enter their credit-card information for purchase. If they clicked "No thanks," it redirected them to another page that offered them just the replay for $9.

The outcome was something I had hoped for but hadn't expected. We added 83 people to the live list and more than doubled our revenue within 12 hours of the email. If all the icing on the cake weren't great enough, we added some sprinkles on top by pitching the experts' paid membership at the end of the live training using my affiliate link, which meant that for every person who attended the call who signed up for the experts' membership programs, I would earn $30 a month until they cancelled.

Upsells and downsells are a genius way to automate additional sales or help you make a sale after a person has turned down your initial offer. With an upsell, you have already gotten someone to purchase one thing from you, so if it's the right upsell, it can be a highly effective way to increase revenue. Don't expect 100 percent conversion on the upsell, but strive for a percentage you feel good about. If your conversion is less than 10 percent, rethink the upsell. Test and experiment to find the right upsell.

For one launch, we offered a Facebook ad course as an upsell after people purchased Build a Blissful Business, which 20 percent ended up purchasing. At a later launch, we offered extended coaching as the upsell and only converted 2 percent. Testing different upsells made it clear to us what people were more excited about.

There are many different offers that can be effective. If I were offering training to teach you how to create a masterclass to pitch your offer, a highly effective upsell would be an editable slide deck you could use for your masterclass. This upsell offer would save you time on the next step of creation. If I were a fitness coach selling a 30-day workout program, a logical next offer would be a 30-day supply of protein shakes that could help speed up your results.

After you come up with an upsell idea, you can create a down-sell option that happens immediately, as I just described with my live Access to the Experts example, or you can create an upsell and downsell that happens over time through automated email sequences. For example, if you launch a large group-coaching program and people sign up for your free masterclass but don't buy the program, you can automatically enter them into a new email sequence that will sell them on a different offer with a lower investment in the next few weeks or months. To make this work, make sure you are offering something the person would want. You can also do market research to find out why people didn't pur-chase. Sometimes it's valuable to create a downsell that sells them the first few steps in the program or a training to help prepare them for the larger offer. If you sell products through an affiliate link and are promoting a large bundle of products, the downsell could be just a few of the products to get them started.

One of my most memorable downsell/upsell journeys was with one of my mentors, Jon. I found him through a YouTube ad and signed up for his masterclass. I attended and instantly booked the discovery call—which I knew would be a sales call—but I was interested in learning more. Since I decided not to join the high-ticket program, I got put into a downsell sequence. Over the next couple months, I received emails that led to another masterclass. This masterclass was prerecorded and pitched a course on how to run YouTube ads. It was something I wanted to learn about, and I felt more comfortable at the lower price point. Once I bought the YouTube-ads course, I was then put into an upsell funnel. I continued to receive emails over the next year until I received one promoting another masterclass on the same topic I was originally pitched and turned down. This time I booked the sales call and joined the high-ticket program they were offering. The automated emails allowed for Jon to continuously communicate with me—keeping him in the forefront of my mind—so when I was ready, I bought and bought again. He used the various offers in his product suite to meet me where I was. The automated funnels allowed him to be in it for the long run without really having to spend extra time and brain space on me specifically—and it paid off for him and his team.

There are so many fun and creative ways to try out an upsell and downsell offer, and it is without a doubt an incredible way to automate more income for your business. But don't get overwhelmed! You don't need an upsell or downsell right away. Building your various offers takes time, and an upsell or downsell can wait.

Automation Steps

Your strategically automated funnel is the key to selling while you sleep and getting back hours each day to do more of the things you love. Here is a summary of the steps to build your automated funnel.

1. Identify your offer.

   What you need:

   a. Software to host your offer

   b. A sales page (recommended but not crucial to get started)

   c. A checkout page

   d. A payment-processing system

   e. A confirmation landing page that thanks customers for their purchases and gives them next steps

   f. A CRM system to deliver additional emails for an effective onboarding process for what they have purchased

2. Get clear about who your ideal customer is for this offer.

3. Create a free offer that will give them a quick win or prepare them for your paid offer. If your offer doesn't feel like the logical best next step, then you have the wrong free gift.

   What you will need:

   a. A free gift or training

   b. A CRM system to collect emails and position your offer as the best next step through your email marketing

   c. An "opt-in" landing page where they can trade their email address for the free gift

   d. A "thank you" landing page to thank them and share next steps

4. Create your email-marketing sequence—four to seven emails to send over the next week or two that will get them excited about your offer, with the last being your pitch.

   What you need:

   a. A CRM system to automate those emails

5. Create and then execute your plan for organic or paid traffic to your freebie.

6. Down the road, consider leveraging additional offers as upsells and downsells to increase revenue.

CHAPTER 8

EFFICIENT PROCESSES

In addition to setting up and automating your funnels, you can gain time for yourself by making all your business processes as efficient as possible. When you don't have processes established, you feel more stressed, like there are always a million things to do and keep track of—*because there are.* Tasks like creating content such as social-media posts or getting your blogs repurposed and published not only can take more time but things can fall through the cracks. When I first launched my podcast, my lack of processes prevented me from publishing an episode every week as I had intended. Every Tuesday would roll around and I would think, "Crap, I need an episode for tomorrow," and then likely not get one done, thus leaving my audience without a new episode and feeling like they couldn't count on me to be consistent. By contrast, when I was able to implement a more efficient process and automate as much as possible, I found myself one month ahead with episodes ready to go weeks ahead of time.

When you have processes in place, you operate much differently. You are far more confident. You check things off of your to-do list quicker, with hours to spare in your day. You make fewer errors. Your performance improves. You feel like you have space to breathe and so much more time for the things you want to do, such as creating more YouTube videos or even just treating yourself to a massage.

Consider Henry Ford. He was not the first to invent the automobile. Karl Benz had introduced the first internal-combustion gas-powered car in Germany in 1885. In 1893, Charles and Frank Duryea made the first successful gas-powered car in the United States and set up the first American car-manufacturing company. Henry Ford's first Model A wasn't produced until 1902, and then the Model T in 1908. And after getting so many orders for the Model T, he revolutionized the industry by producing standard interchangeable parts and using conveyor belts to create a moving assembly line.

What made Ford so memorably successful was *not* inventing the car but rather becoming more efficient at production and thereby driving the price of the car down. He recognized which aspects in the automobile-manufacturing process were taking the most time: having groups of just two or three workers assemble each car with workers continually going back and forth to get the parts for the next step to build one car at a time. By using conveyor belts to take each car down the line where each person had their specific role, he was able to increase production quantity and decrease production time. This allowed him to raise revenues and improve working conditions (fewer hours, higher wages). For you, developing and leveraging efficient systems will be the difference between a stressful, unproductive business and a business with few mistakes, high performance, and more personal free time.

As an online business owner today, you have thousands of ways you can leverage efficient processes and automation. As with any typical business, there are going to be regular tasks that need to happen: content to create, people to engage with, appointments to schedule. Though it's important that you come up with your own processes that work, I will give you some tips that have helped me, a squirrel-brained, can't-stay-organized-if-my-life-depended-on-it, I-just-wanna-have-fun kind of CEO. These systems allow me to appear to the outside world as a naturally put-together, she-loves-to-be-organized kind of person. Yes, you need to make a conscious effort to set up efficient and, whenever possible, automated systems, but it is 100 percent worth it. Without it, there is no way I could have generated the kind of success I've had while working less than 20 hours a week.

Key Concepts in Efficiency

Systems and Processes

You may be wondering, "What's the difference between systems and processes?" Let me explain. Systems are the core elements you use to provide goods or services to your customer—the "what" of your offer, which stems from the value you intend to provide to your customer. On the other hand, processes are the things you do to make your systems work more efficiently—the "how" of your business.

You may not think you have a particular system or process because you have never thought about it, but you may already have one. Take a task you do from start to finish, such as creating a blog post. The blog post is a system you use to drive traffic to your offer. The process would spell out the steps needed to create and maintain your blog post. Think about the order in which you do any given part of your business. Write down that process step by step. The best way to make your business efficient is to look for any systems (parts of creating and selling your offer) that take you a long time and look for a process to make them more efficient. Once you have spelled out a process, think about how you can modify it to make it even more efficient. Time-blocking or batch-creating can be areas that allow you to make your processes more efficient.

Time-Blocking and Batch Creation

Time-blocking refers to blocking off time on your calendar and dedicating it to a particular task or project. For example, you can block off three one-hour time blocks to focus on emails, engage on social media, and create your course. Batch creation is when you dedicate your time to creating a large amount of similar content in one sitting. For example, you can batch-create a year's worth of monthly emails in one sitting. Batch creation can be highly effective for tasks such as creating social-media content. Instead of creating one social post every day, sit down and create all your social posts for the following week.

Time-blocking and batch creation are incredible ways to get more done in less time. Why? Studies show that it takes 10 to 15 minutes to get into a flow of work.[4] "Flow" is a state of being in which you aren't distracted by the things around you and you become hyperefficient in what you are doing. For us ADHDers (undiagnosed here, but I highly relate!), it can be quite challenging to get into a flow state.

Imagine that you sit down to work for an hour and it takes you 15 minutes to get into a flow state. That gives you just 45 minutes of real, channeled, efficient work done. If you did this Monday through Thursday (because you are running your business with a keep-Fridays-open mentality), this would be four hours of work per week but only three hours of actual, efficient work completed. If you have a difficult time getting into a flow state, consider scheduling larger chunks of time to work.

Time-blocking was the most efficient way for me to get this book written. I tried scheduling two hours a few times a week, but I realized that once I got into a flow state, I wanted to keep writing. Whenever I would have to stop for another obligation, I became frustrated as doing so meant it would take me that much longer to write. I changed my time blocks to five-hour chunks one day a week and was able to be much more efficient.

PRO TIP

Time-blocking and batch-creating for similar content are great ways to increase efficiency. For example, block off two hours just to create your week's worth of short-form videos for Instagram Reels and YouTube shorts. Then block off another two hours to write your weekly emails. Then block four hours another day to record your long-form podcast and YouTube videos. Test different ways of structuring your tasks and see when you are most efficient. Everyone will be a little different, so the goal is to test it out and discover what makes you the most efficient and then stick with the process that works best for you.

I prefer to record multiple podcast episodes back to back. And if I am the one editing my episodes, scheduling their release, and creating the marketing emails, I'd rather record and edit immediately and then schedule and craft the marketing email before moving on to the next episode. Any areas that I know need to be edited are fresh in my mind and make the process a lot faster. This is a time when I break my "batch similar content" strategy and batch-create content for a particular topic. For many other tasks, such as creating social-media posts or emails for a funnel, I like to focus on one thing before I move on. This allows me to become hyperefficient as my brain is focused on one task on repeat and I don't have to switch back and forth between different creative aspects.

Flowcharts

Once you develop a process for something, write it down! This will not only help keep you organized but also allow someone else to understand the process when needed. If you are a visual person, flowcharts are a great way to visualize your process in its entirety. You can also use flowcharts to show the flow of something, such as a funnel.

As a solopreneur, these charts help keep everything from your onboarding processes to funnels organized. Your business will start out simple, but over the years, your content will grow, your offerings will expand, and your team will get larger. Having a step-by-step list of what happens in your process or a flowchart that shows the steps of your funnel will allow you to stay on track. When you start to hire team members, it will speed up the training process and make it more organized.

We use flowcharts to visualize our product suite and sales processes with upsells and downsells. Doing the same will help you or your tech assistant set up offers, upsells, and downsells, along with linking up the appropriate email sequences with fewer errors. It will also save you from being overwhelmed by chaos should you need to step away and let someone else take over. Life is unpredictable and happens at the most inopportune times.

Canva is a great program to use if you want to create a visual graphics-based flowchart. Below is an example of one I created to keep our podcasting process organized. You can use flowcharts as a reference for yourself and also to train your team. When I switched assistants, this saved me a tremendous amount of time getting her up to speed with the steps in the system. We call these SOPs (standard operating processes), and we keep a folder in our Google Drive labeled "SOPs."

PODCAST—STANDARD OPERATING PROCESS

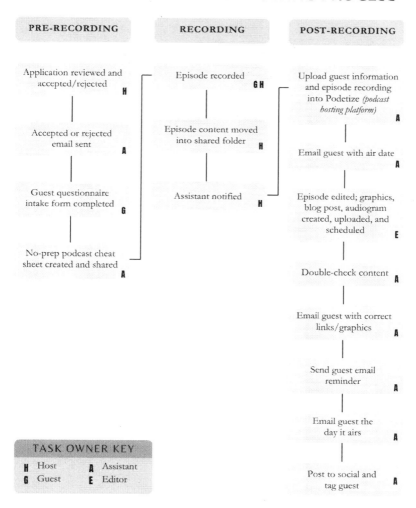

PRE-RECORDING

Application reviewed and accepted/rejected **H**

Accepted or rejected email sent **A**

Guest questionnaire intake form completed **G**

No-prep podcast cheat sheet created and shared **A**

RECORDING

Episode recorded **G H**

Episode content moved into shared folder **H**

Assistant notified **H**

POST-RECORDING

Upload guest information and episode recording into Podetize *(podcast hosting platform)* **A**

Email guest with air date **A**

Episode edited; graphics, blog post, audiogram created, uploaded, and scheduled **E**

Double-check content **A**

Email guest with correct links/graphics **A**

Send guest email reminder **A**

Email guest the day it airs **A**

Post to social and tag guest **A**

TASK OWNER KEY

H	Host	**A**	Assistant
G	Guest	**E**	Editor

This quick visual allows anyone to step in and review the flow of our process and implement it.

SOP Lists

A step-by-step list of your process can also come in handy. Though this could be a visual built in Canva, you can also simply use Google Sheets or any table to add your steps. Here is an example of part of the steps in our podcasting process with clickable links (noted by underlined words) for quick access to important trainings and documents.

BADASS IS THE NEW BLACK PODCAST
STANDARD OPERATING PROCESS

TASK	TASK OWNER	DUE DATE	TRAINING VIDEO	LINKS NEEDED
Application reviewed *Notify VA via email if accepted or rejected*	Host	ASAP		
Email the applicant to accept or reject their application	Virtual Assistant (VA)	ASAP		"Applicant Approved" email Or "Applicant Rejected" email
Guest questionnaire intake form completed	Guest	7 days		
Follow up with the guest if they don't complete within a week	VA	ASAP	Click here to watch	"Guest Questionnaire reminder" email
Prep for the episode: 1. Fill out the No-Prep Podcast Cheat Sheet and post episode notes 2. Create a folder with the guest name inside the "Episodes Completed" folder 3. Share No-Prep Podcast Cheat Sheet to Hosts@email.com for viewing	VA	ASAP	Click here to watch	No-Prep Cheat Sheet template Google Form to view results Episodes Completed Folder
Record episode: 1. Record episode 2. Complete the Post Episode Prep 3. Move recording into the guest's folder 4. Move No-Prep Cheat Sheet and post episode notes into guests folder 5. Notify VA via ClickUp when completed	Host	ASAP		
Upload episode information into podcast platform (Podetize)	VA	ASAP	Click here to watch	Podetize login

Templates

Sign up for or buy pre-built templates to use to get the job done quicker. If you are trying to launch an offer and need a sales page, you could spend hours upon hours creating from scratch, *or* you could buy a template that will give you the copy outline to fill in your content and a pre-built page predesigned for you to insert your copy. Anytime you can find a pre-built template to use as a starting point, it will help you create faster. It's one of the reasons we launched a template shop for our community. We want to take you from start to finish faster.

Once again, Canva is a great place to find thousands of graphic templates to help you get started. There is a free version, but the pro version will give you a lot more flexibility for design. This can be a huge time-saver in creating social graphics, YouTube thumbnail images, or even PDFs such as checklists or guides for your freebie.

Calendars

Using an appointment-booking system such as Calendly or AcuityScheduling can save you and your clients a ton of time and hassle. Before having a calendar system, I found myself emailing and texting back and forth with people trying to figure out what the best time was to schedule a meeting or podcast recording. I would text a few dates and times and then they would respond saying that those didn't work. They would respond with a few options and those wouldn't work for me. It was a constant back-and-forth that sometimes lasted days.

After you finally agree on a date and time, both parties then must add it to their calendar and remember to show up. As the host, you then have to craft an email to send the other party your Zoom link and any other information they need. A lot can fall through the cracks. Imagine that you get this message right as the kids are getting off the bus and you have a full afternoon of snacks, homework, and sports practice ahead of you. By the time you have a free minute, you have completely forgotten that you have to email the link and information. Days go by and the recording time arrives. You scramble to get your guest the information and when they show, they have not taken a shower and are without a freebie offer prepared, not realizing you were supposed to repurpose the video for YouTube. Everyone is flustered, your guest is frustrated, and you have not made the best impression.

Instead, leverage a calendar to make booking with you easy and automate sending any information that people will need to get prepared. You can customize your calendar to block out certain dates and times and even sync it to your personal calendar so if you add a personal appointment, it will block off the time on your client-booking calendar to ensure you don't double book. You can even have different links for different kinds of appointments. For example, when someone books on my calendar to be a guest on my podcast, it blocks off 60 minutes. When a student books time to record a testimonial with me, it only blocks off 30 minutes. When I set up a meet-and-greet to talk about collaboration, it blocks off 40 minutes.

The calendar software also allows for your clients to reschedule if needed with a simple link inside their calendar event. You can also leverage the automated emails to send instructions and your link to join you to meet. It can also send reminder emails the day before or the day of an event to increase attendance rates. This will allow for a seamless process and will win over your audience and make you the most organized and professional person they know! I have heard time and time again, "This was such a seamless process; you are so organized. I love it!" Little do they know that I'm the least-organized person around and it's the automation saving me on the daily. Setting up calendars and integrating them into your website will save you hours of work every day and make you look like a total badass.

Prescheduling Content

Once you have all your content created, prescheduling is the icing on the cake. It significantly saves you time, streamlines your workflow, and eliminates the need for last-minute scrambling. Prescheduling is like having your own virtual assistant making sure emails get sent, social posts get posted on time, and videos go live when they are supposed to.

When we offer new enrollments into Build a Blissful Business, we usually go all out in promotion. We send marketing emails, launch podcast episodes, and post to social media. In one of our six-figure launches, we posted three times over two weeks. It wasn't due to a lack of content. We had created 10 social posts, but I didn't preschedule any of them. Once the launch kicked off, I was so busy monitoring other things with the launch, as well as the day-to-day care of my family, that posting on social media ended up being the thing that got dropped.

Prescheduling allows you to keep consistent contact even when you are unavailable (think maternity leave) and take advantage of peak engagement times by scheduling content when your target audience is most active. If your audience is most active at 6:00 p.m. but you're busy making dinner, there is no way you can post during that time. By using a prescheduler such as Later, Planoly, or Tailwind, you can maximize the reach and impact of your messages.

Many platforms allow you to preschedule your content directly. You can schedule YouTube videos right inside YouTube and Facebook videos inside Facebook. However, some third-party software, such as Metricoll, allows you to preschedule *and* cross-post, meaning you can create a piece of short-form content, upload it into the software, and instruct the software to post the content to Instagram, Facebook, and TikTok at the same time. This allows you to show up across multiple platforms with little effort. By automating this process, you will free up time to focus on other important aspects of your business, such as client interactions, strategic planning, and creative endeavors.

When you use these strategies, techniques, and software, you will find yourself able to get an incredible amount of work done in less time. You will be able to create and share more content and build a reputation for always being on top of things.

AI

Thank goodness I dragged my feet for two years on writing this book because I get to add this section about AI without having to do a revision! But seriously, AI is all the rage and developing at a rapid rate. You may fear that AI is going to take over and that there will be no reason for someone to buy your course on how to knit a dog sweater. Don't worry, though; AI isn't going to take your place. AI can't take away your opinions, perspective, life experience, or personality—or the deep human connection you have with your community. It can, however, help you do things more efficiently, such as creating a course outline and lessons, writing content, making original music, taking notes on a masterclass you can't attend live, editing videos or images, or turning a 60-minute video into three short promotional clips—all within minutes. There are many helpful ways to use AI to help you be hyperefficient.

AI levels the playing field and can give anyone who wants to use it the opportunity to start at a five instead of a zero. Imagine sitting down to write a blog post. You have a topic idea, but you are starting from scratch. You aren't in the mood to write. Not a single creative atom is bouncing around your brain. You have no idea where to start and fear that this blog is going to take your entire morning. With AI, it can take you from a zero to a five within minutes. Access ChatGPT or Jasper and type in, "Write me a blog post about the top 10 kid-friendly resorts around the world with childcare that still provide a luxurious experience," and in 30 seconds it will spit out a blog post. This gives you a starting point to research and the context may remind you of a story you want to include in the blog.

AI can spit out a blog post in under one minute, but you will still need to review and make your revisions. Add your own voice to it (even though the more you use an AI platform, the more it adjusts to your voice) and incorporate examples that come to mind or stories from your experience. This makes the content interesting and engaging and helps your readers get to know you more and form a deeper connection with you through your stories. AI has no way of knowing your personal story about the time you took your kids to a resort expecting to use the childcare services so you could have adult time and then realized the age minimum for daycare was four years old but your youngest was three. Unfortunately, you had a very honest three-year-old who, when asked their age, said, "I'm fwee," holding up three tiny fingers. You were quickly called away from your relaxing beach chair to come get your child. (True story that happened to my sister at our wedding in Mexico.)

If you are leveraging time-blocking to batch-create four You-Tube videos or podcasts, you could type in "give me 10 video ideas for YouTube to teach a brick-and-mortar business how to create better systems" or "give me a list of 20 things new pet owners struggle with when getting their first puppy." AI is going to spit out some ideas in under 30 seconds. You can take your own knowledge and decide which videos make the most sense for you to create. If you are anything like me, it sometimes takes you forever to decide on what to write or record, but once you have the topic, it's easy to share your knowledge and stories. AI gives you the jump-start you need to speed up the process of whatever it is you are doing. It really takes you from a zero to a five in seconds so you can get to a 10, a finished product, in half the time.

There are so many ways I am using AI to save hours of time. Here are just a few topics and tools to help you start entertaining the idea of incorporating AI into your content-creation systems and processes.

Picture Editing

Fotor: best overall AI photo editor
Luminar Neo: best AI photo editor for PC
Pixlr: best AI photo editor for creative editing
Let's Enhance: best AI photo editor for e-commerce
Befunky: best online AI photo editor for beginners

Podcast Editing

Capsho uses AI to help you create your podcast assets. Upload an audio file and in under 10 minutes, it creates your episode title, description, show notes, social posts, promotional email, blog post, YouTube description, and a full transcript.

Cast Magic is similar and can create show notes, summaries, social posts, and a transcript.

Voice
WellSaid Labs can take typed text and turn it into a voice audio of your voice.

Copywriting
Copywriting has never been easier than with new AI platforms that can write creative stories to depict your point, improve grammar, and offer concise options as well as highlight potential grammar mistakes, typos, or inconsistencies in your copy. These AI platforms can also generate compelling phrases, headlines, or content concepts to inspire your copywriting process. I love using **ChatGPT** and **Jasper** to help me get started with my copy. I then use **Grammarly** to proofread copy, fix misspelled words, and make grammar suggestions to improve my writing.

Photo Editing
So much of our online world is visual. You may not have gone to photography school, but with the help of the high-tech, built-in cameras on your smartphone and photo editing, you can appear professional. Here are some platforms that make photo editing a breeze.

Uizard
Designs.ai
Adobe Sensei
Fronty
AutoDraw

Khroma
Let's Enhance
Jasper Art

Note-Taking

Bummed you missed a meeting or live webinar? Now you can be in two places at once with AI. There are several platforms that attend a meeting for you and transcribe in real time.

Otter.ai: records audio, transcribes, and summarizes.
MeetGeek.ai: record, transcribe, and share.
Sembly.ai: upload past meetings, search by keywords, and send sembly.ai to your meeting for you to take notes, summarize, and more.
Fireflies.ai: transcribes, summarizes, and analyzes voice conversations.

Autoresponders (Chatbots)

Though it may feel impersonal to have an autoresponder when someone comments on your social posts or sends you a message, it may be the difference between someone getting the information they want and being left high and dry. Before using AI to auto-respond, I would notice an old social post where I said, "Comment 'YES' below and I'll send you the link." I can't tell you how many times I've gotten a random notification and realized five people had typed "YES" weeks before but I had never sent the information.

Considering that this is often the first step in your automated funnel, it's important to focus on two things:

1. Eliminating as many barriers as you can that prevent people from acting.
2. Eliminating as much work for yourself as possible.

You can leverage chatbots such as Manychat to eliminate the barriers. Long gone are the days when you'd say, "Use the 'link in bio' to download my free checklist," at the end of a social-media post or video. This call to action requires your viewers to leave the post they are looking at, click into your bio, and sift through links to find the right one. With simple software such as Manychat, you can give a call to action that says, "Type 'ABS' in the comments and I'll send you the link to my 15-minute six-pack-abs workout." Manychat will then recognize any comment with "abs" and automatically send them a direct message (DM) with a link you crafted ahead of time as well as reply to their comment to let them know you have just sent them information. This literally takes less than 10 minutes to set up to be able to respond to thousands of people while you are eating tasty tacos with your bestie on a Tuesday afternoon.

There are two benefits to this strategy. One, it sends the inquirer the appropriate link, instantly giving them access right when they're most interested, making them more likely to act. Two, it causes them to comment on your post in order to get what they want, which tells a platform such as Instagram that your content is getting attention and helps push your content to more people.

You can use this to drive traffic to your freebie or straight to a paid offer.

I was lying awake in bed at 1:00 a.m. scrolling Instagram when I spotted a post promoting a private podcast episode sharing someone's seven-figure strategy using AI, and I could listen for just $9. If I wanted access, I had to comment with the keyword "'AI,'" and she would send me the information. Of course, I did so, curious as to how this was going to play out, and I instantly received a message saying, "I'm so pumped you want to listen to my new private podcast! You also get to ask questions and I will answer them in a new episode! Click to access for just $9." A button was right below the text.

I guarantee she was *not* lying awake stalking her Instagram comments to then copy and paste that message to me. She was using Manychat to do the task work for her.

I clicked on the button that read "Click to learn more" because $9 felt like a no-brainer. Of course, when I landed on the checkout page, there was the option to add on a spreadsheet with the full breakdown for an additional $18. Because I am a sucker for a cheap upsell, I added it to my cart and hit purchase. This automation allowed her to wake up to two new sales from yours truly. I love that for her!

It feels *great* to sell while you sleep!

Imagine if she didn't have the response automated and I had to wait until the next day to receive the link with information; it would have gotten lost in a hundred other messages, and she would have lost two valuable sales. Plus, it eliminated her having to do the physical work of grabbing the link and sending me the message herself.

Learning AI and building your systems and processes takes time. To get started feeling less overwhelmed, identify one thing in your business that you do repeatedly and write down your process. See if there is any way to refine it or incorporate more AI to automate tasks. Before you know it, you will have a folder of organized SOPs and will be savvy in a variety of AI software.

PART III

BUSINESS FUNDAMENTALS TO HELP YOU GROW AND SCALE

CHAPTER 9

SMART HIRING PRACTICES

Do you ever think to yourself, "Ugh, I just don't have time for this"? I know you have. We all have. As your business grows, you will find yourself chanting this phrase more and more. Either you will not have time for certain tasks and they won't get done or you will find yourself doing work-related things during family time.

I realized I needed to hire additional help when I found myself working every evening. Bonding time with my hubby became catching-up-on-work time. I felt like I didn't have time to do any of the things I used to enjoy doing—such as lying down to watch a show before bed with my husband.

I started this business so I could have more time and freedom, not to be a slave to my own business! The moment I laid down in bed one evening and my husband said, "Accepting people into the group again?" was the moment I realized I needed to hire help.

It was crystal clear that I needed to hire for this part of my workload. I was doing the same task repeatedly, manually verifying that those who were requesting to join our Facebook group were paying customers. Anyone could handle this task for our business, so why was I still doing it? I immediately reached out to a chat group, got a recommendation for a potential hire, and had someone onboard within a week to take it over. This was the start of our team of 16.

If you can't automate it, then hire for it.

I bet you're thinking, "Well, of course, I would love to hire someone, but I don't have the money for that." But think about it this way: can you afford *not* to hire someone? When you find yourself trapped in the day-to-day of your business—responding to emails and setting up new automation, payables, receivables—it really can be the death of you and your business. Plus, this doesn't need to be a full-time employee. In fact, it probably shouldn't be to start. You can hire independent contractors per project or for a limited amount of time until you get to the place where you need more help.

I have worked with many clients who got into business to help people and make a difference. They loved working with them but quickly realized they would need to put on a variety of other "hats" if they really wanted to turn their side hustle into a profitable and scalable business.

If what you are doing on a daily basis is making you hate your business or is not allowing you to do the things that help you grow your revenue, then I would say you can't afford *not* to hire help. Running a successful business doesn't mean you need to grow a team of 15. It all depends on the nature of your business. However,

I will say that I have never met a single entrepreneur making multiple six figures who has never hired one ounce of help. It's time to hire when there is just too much for one person to do. Even after you have automated everything you can, you will still find that there are some things only a human can do.

My friend and mentor Graham Cochrane is a great example of being able to run a very successful business—actually, two seven-figure businesses—while only working five hours a week and with only a couple people he's hired to help him. He has been able to do this with a strategic product suite. The offers build off one another, and he has kept his business model very simple.

At some point, you will come to a crossroads where you feel you just can't take on another thing, or you might see your business start to stall or even backslide because you have taken on too much and haven't been able to focus your efforts on the things that move the needle forward. When that time comes—or maybe you are already there—I want you to be prepared and understand what positions to hire, how to find the best candidates, and how to bring on the right people for the job.

What to Hire Out

First, you must be honest about what goes on in your business. The best way to do that is to sit down with pen and paper (or keyboard if you want to get digital) and make a list of everything you do in your business. I'm talking about everything from sharpening pencils to answering emails, booking calls, and writing content. You can even include the things that have to be taken care of to allow you to work: caring for your children, cooking dinner, prepping lunches, driving to sports practices. If you do it, jot it down. Then write down the things that aren't getting done because you don't have time or the skill set.

Once you are done creating your list, you are going to Marie Kondo the crap out of it! Yup, totally used her name as a verb. Though Marie Kondo became popular for helping people tidy up their homes, I want you to use her principles to help you tidy up your business. As Marie Kondo would say, "If it doesn't spark joy, let it go."[5]

Take the list of everything you do in your business and life and, in red ink, slash out everything that doesn't spark joy. If you hate doing it, you avoid it, or it's getting in the way of what you really want to be doing, it gets a big, fat red line through it. (The reason I like this exercise is that everyone finds joy in different things. I could tell you five things to hire for, but if one of those things lights you up and you're no longer doing it, you may not find yourself feeling the same level of joy in your business as you did before. Joy is one thing you need as an entrepreneur to help you get through the tough days.)

Once this is done, it's time to look at your list and put a big, fat X through anything you just cannot do because your skill set isn't there. It could be taking professional photos, designing a website, or drawing something spectacular. Now circle five to 10 things that take up the most of your time.

Here is where the magic happens. The things you listed that have a red slash *and* a circle around them are going to be the first things you consider hiring for. Imagine if you farmed out to someone else the things that you hate and are incredibly time consuming.

Now, it's time to start small. Most people don't decide they need help and then hire five people the next day. It's a gradual process. You start with one and grow as you need and can.

Looking at your list, what seems the most feasible thing to hire for?

If you have five things that feel equally time consuming and hated but you can't hire a contractor to help right now, think about some of these other factors to help you determine which might be the first thing you hire for.

➢ How easily could you find someone to take this over?

➢ What is the easiest to train someone on?

➢ What is the cost?

Also consider the things you listed that you could not do and put a big red X through. How important are these things? Are they preventing you from moving forward in other areas of your business? Are they causing you to lose money? If so, these are also going to be high on the list of priorities to hire for.

If it would be easy to find someone and train them and it wouldn't cause too much financial strain, then this could be your answer to "what do I hire for first?" If it takes a larger investment but the ROI is greater, then it is worth handing over to someone else.

Our very first hire was a photographer. We just didn't possess the skill set to take the beautiful pictures we would need to launch our offer, so it was a no-brainer for us.

Our next hire was an assistant so I could be more efficient and effective with my time. I had the daunting task of admitting our new members into the community Facebook group. We had about 60 people requesting access a day, all of whom needed to be verified before being admitted. I was doing the same thing over and over again every single night, taking up my whole evening, and found no joy in it. Plus, it was taking time away from my husband. I loved our quiet evenings together after the kids went down, so having to do work felt like my business was putting me in a cage rather than giving me wings.

One evening, I texted Claire: "We have got to find someone to hire to do this job. It's not that hard, I don't think it would cost much, and it would be easy for me to show someone how to do it." This was the true catalyst for building a larger team in just a few years.

I call this type of hiring process the "entrepreneur hire." You hire based on tasks that need to get done. Though this can be effective at the start, the idea is to transition into the role of CEO of your business and you hire based on what is best for the company, which may be different from what is best for you.

Do you have an entrepreneur or a CEO mindset?

Assume that Sally is maxed out with her daily tasks and supporting her current clients and feels like she has no time to grow her business. She is signing up one new client a month and making $60,000 annually, but she wants to grow her business to $1 million annually. She only has time to spend three hours a month to take three sales calls in order to land a new client. She knows that, at this rate, she is never going to build a million-dollar business. Having performed the exercise, she looks at her list of tasks—the ones she has slashed out, X-ed out, and circled—and decides that she needs to hire an administrator to help her with such day-to-day tasks as checking and replying to emails. She can only afford to hire one person for five hours a week. This would allow her to take 12 sales calls a month, which would bump her up to four clients a month. Her business would quadruple, which she believes would put her on her way to building the empire she imagines. But there is *one* major piece she is forgetting to take into consideration before deciding what to hire for: she is not thinking like a CEO.

As an entrepreneur, you think more "in the moment" and make reactionary decisions. Something happens, so you make a decision. You have tasks you don't like to do so you hire help, just like we talked about. Though there is nothing wrong with this, I want to take you to the next level and help you think like a CEO, because hiring like a CEO will help you grow your business 10 times faster than you could ever imagine.

A CEO thinks less in the moment and more about the future. Instead of making decisions in reaction to some problem, a CEO plans and makes decisions based on *where they want to go*.

With a CEO mentality, you will think about hiring based on where you want your business to go, not just about what can be taken off your plate. Where do you want your business to be in one year, five years, 10 years? Though you might not have any darn clue (which is common among entrepreneurs), a CEO thinks about the business's future and hires based on where they want it to go.

Let's go back to Sally, the woman who wants to scale her $60,000-a-year business to $1 million. Now thinking like a

CEO, she knows that she needs to take more sales calls. She focuses on her end goal of growing her business to $1 million annually, thinks about what it would take to do that, and realizes she will need to sign 18 new clients a month. If she continues to close at 33 percent, she will need to take 55 sales calls during that time. Now, hiring one admin to take over some tasks isn't going to give her an extra 52 hours a month to take on that many additional sales calls, but she knows that this is what is needed to grow her business. Sally, thinking like a CEO, decides to hire another salesperson instead.

The additional salesperson will immediately take on the extra sales calls that Sally would have had to turn down, and she can now grow her business fivefold almost immediately. This also allows her to have more capital to hire an admin to take over certain tasks in her business, freeing up her time to spend finding more potential customers to fill her funnel. In other words, the admin support allows her to fill her funnel, and a full funnel keeps her new salesperson busy taking calls to convert customers and bring in revenue.

In this scenario, Sally takes the time to think about not only what needs to be taken off her plate but also the future of her business. Thinking like a CEO allows her to make the best hiring moves to cause the needle to jump the most.

Though you should 100 percent make a list of all the things you do and then determine what you don't like doing, what takes the most time, and what you can't do, don't forget to think like a CEO and hire based on where you are trying to go. Sometimes hiring out a little support for simple tasks still makes the most sense.

It's like basketball. An entrepreneur is stuck on defense, having to make quick decisions to prevent the other team from scoring. Thinking like a CEO, on the other hand, is like playing offense: You are methodically dribbling the ball down the court as the rest of the team rushes down to help score a basket. You are thinking ahead about what plays you have been practicing that could get you the outcome you want. You take your time to set it up just right so you can make the winning shot.

I also encourage you to think about what you will do with the new time you gain once you've hired help. If you hire for a task that takes you five hours, what could you do with those newfound five hours that could help bring in more revenue for the business? Be sure to replace the time with something that will help move the business forward. Maybe Sally decides to use the five extra hours a week to create a digital course that will allow her to bring in another revenue stream for her business, getting her to her $1 million year even faster with fewer sales calls.

Though sometimes you will need to hire based on tasks that need to get done, having a forward-thinking approach to hiring based on where you want your business to go will be the big difference between coasting to the finish line in the middle of the pack on a bicycle and strapping a motor on that bad boy, putting the pedal to the metal, and finishing first. Running your business like a CEO will not only be your ticket to scaling but will also be what sets you apart from the rest and helps you build a profitable and *blissful* business.

Common Roles for Hiring

Virtual assistant tasks: These could be anything from answering your support questions to responding to common emails.

Bookkeeping and accounting: It's incredibly important to keep track of your business expenses and how much is going out versus coming in. I recommend a weekly look at your profit and loss (P&L) statement to keep a steady pulse on the business. A weekly check allows you to course correct before it's too late. If this is a part of the CEO role that stops you dead in your tracks, find a way to hire for it. A good accountant can often find a way to save you enough money to essentially cover what they cost you to employ them. Don't forget that you can write off their fee as an expense too.

Copywriter: A copywriter is someone who will write for you. You could hire a copywriter to write social-media content, blog posts, marketing emails, website pages, and sales pages. It's important to ask potential copywriting hires exactly what kind of copy they write. If you are looking for someone to create content for a sales page to sell your offer, then you will want to look for someone who writes conversion copy. This is very different from someone who writes blog posts and general marketing material. There is a science and psychology to sales and conversion copy.

Good copywriters can be on the expensive side, so if you can learn how to write effective copy yourself, you'll save the business a lot of money. However, if it's not your zone of genius, then it might be time to hire someone. You could pay them hourly, or you could hire them per project, which can have a wide range in cost. I have seen some very experienced writers charge as much as $10,000 a day. Ultimately, you need to factor in how much you need to have written, whether is it ongoing or just a one-time project, how much can you afford, and how much such an investment will bring back into the business.

Graphic designer. This is someone who would make visuals for you such as a business card, a free guide, pictures for your course or presentation, or a logo. Designers are also more expensive than a typical virtual assistant as they have a skill and talent not every person can just learn. A do-it-yourself alternative is the easy-to-use program Canva, which allows nongraphic designers to do graphic-design work. Canva has hundreds of templates created by professional designers that you can use as a starting point.

Website designer. A website designer is a bit different from a graphic designer, although the same person could likely fill both roles. There is a lot of strategy behind a website design because it helps create a positive experience for the customer. It is also used as a tool to drive traffic to different areas. When you don't take these things into consideration, your user can feel overwhelmed by your website design and leave without taking action, costing you revenue. Make sure that when you hire a website designer, they know and understand websites and how the design can impact the customer journey. Note that whenever you hire for a design project, the copy will need to be written beforehand. If you have a project that needs both, either find someone who has a team to cover both copy and design, like us, or know that you will need to have your copy completed before the design work can be done. Changing the copy can drastically change the design, so don't submit website copy to a designer if you plan to change the content. Make sure it is ready to go before the design project starts.

Social-media manager. This is someone who would manage your social media. This person could potentially write your social media or, if you have a copywriter who writes for you, just manage the posting.

Project manager/integrator. This person could also be referred to as an OBM (online business manager) and is someone who will take your ideas and goals for the business and put a plan together to reach them. They will then oversee the projects at hand.

Where to Find Good Hires

Turn to your community. We have found some great hires right from our own community. We just crafted a job description and then posted it in the Facebook group and emailed it out.

Ask your network. I have found many of my hires simply by asking friends in my industry who they are using or if they have a referral for someone they know who's looking for work in the area I need. When people recommend others they have previously worked and had a good experience with, it increases the chances you will also have a good experience.

Use hiring websites. Popular sites such as Indeed, Fiverr, Upwork, and ZipRecruiter are good places to post job positions and find reliable freelance workers or employees.

Tips for the Perfect Hire

Write down the skills and traits for the positions you need (and don't forget soft skills such as people skills, communication skills, listening skills, time management, problem-solving, leadership, and empathy—and making sure you are aligned with that person from a values standpoint). Have it next to you every time you look at a résumé or conduct an interview and let it guide you in your hiring decisions. Don't hire the candidate whom you relate to the most or who will do the job just like you. In fact, look to hire people who are going to do the job better than you. Hire those who compensate for and complement your weaknesses. As a visionary, I needed my integrator to be incredibly organized and analytical (traits that don't come naturally to me). Our integrator is 100 percent those things, which allows her to thrive in her role. Look for team players and those who are eager and efficient.

Hire slow and fire fast. There will come a point in time when you will have hired someone who doesn't work out. Either the quality of their work isn't good, they have a bad attitude, or you just don't need their services anymore. Firing is hard, even if it's a part-time contractor, but remember, it's not personal—it's business, and there is nothing worse for your business than paying for services that are not effective or helping it grow.

CHAPTER 10

COMMON MISTAKES TO AVOID

I was at the height of my career. The money was cascading in. Paying off my credit card in full every single month left plenty to spare. Every time I looked at my bank account, my checking account was growing. It was the most incredible feeling I had ever had. There had been so many moments in my life when I was living paycheck to paycheck. I remember being in college and working three jobs, always feeling like I couldn't get ahead. Even after college, when my income doubled, it still felt impossible to get ahead. It was the perpetual feeling of, "*How am I ever going to pay off all my school debt? At this rate, it seems like it's going to take a hundred years.*"

But now that was all in the past. Claire and I were making over $2,000 a day in our digital business. There wasn't a day we didn't have new people joining our membership. I felt unstoppable and excited for the future.

My husband, Michael, and I had been talking for years about purchasing a lake house. Every time we hopped in the car to go to our friend's lake house, we talked through what it would be like to have one of our own and how much we needed to increase our income each month to make that dream a reality. At that point, I was bringing in twice what we needed every month.

The moment we closed on the lake house, we celebrated with Mexican food and ice-cold margaritas. The celebratory reverberation of our glasses clinking still replays in my head. (I'm literally driving to the lake house as I voice memo this chapter—and it feels so good!) The sun is beaming through the windshield of my Tesla so brightly that I need both my sunglasses and my visor to see the road ahead of me.

I can remember the feelings of excitement and awe that we were "doing it." Claire and I were making a ridiculous amount of money. We had surpassed the $2 million mark in our business, we were incredibly profitable, and every month the business grew. *I was successful!*

Then this conversation kept happening.

Michael would ask me, "How's the business going?"

Me: "It's great!"

Michael: "How many members joined this month?"

Me: "I don't know." (in a bit of a shy tone)

Michael: "How many members cancelled this month?"

Me: "I don't know, but we're making more money every single month!" (feeling the need to quickly defend myself)

In the beginning of building my business, whenever my husband would ask me questions or give me advice, it would make me feel like I wasn't a good business owner, as if he were telling me I was doing it wrong. After some internal personal development (which could be the subject of a whole other book), I realized that he was only trying to help. Every time he would ask me about my business and the numbers and I didn't have a good response, I would shut down. I would change the subject. I would tell myself, *"It's fine. Your business is growing. You're looking at the numbers; it looks good, and it feels good."*

The pandemic came. The money was still flowing in. We had just given out a few raises. We had 14 contractors working for us. I was only spending about two to three hours a week in one business and five hours a week in the other one. It felt like, pandemic or no pandemic, nothing was going to stop us. My dream life had become my real life. *Success!*

But then it all changed. The year 2022 came and, suddenly, the numbers weren't going up. It seemed like overnight our business had dropped substantially. However, I realize now that had I been paying attention to the numbers like a real CEO should have, I would've seen it coming long beforehand.

Claire and I were no longer making $2,000 a day. We weren't signing up new customers every day. In fact, we weren't making enough to pay ourselves. Thankfully, we had done a good job of saving along the way, but this wasn't how we wanted to use our savings. The savings were for investments that were going to make us more money, not to pay us monthly. Our membership had dropped, our contractor costs were sky high, and—though it actually happened over a period of time—it seemed like the downturn had happened overnight.

I sat down at my office desk on the first of the month, afraid to open our P&L to see what our monthly profits would be. It was not a happy day. Apparently, I needed to learn the importance of tracking the data the hard way.

What happened? How the heck were we going to recover? All the confidence I had built about being a successful business owner had shattered like a vase, hitting the floor in slow motion. *Who was going to trust me to help them build their business when mine was crashing to the ground?*

There were a number of reasons why the numbers were regressing; it wasn't just one thing that could easily be fixed. It was a multitude of factors, some which were out of my control, such as an increase to the cost of ads. However, there were others I could fix, such as the number of contractors we were paying and shifting the product model to support what our customers wanted now, which, like much of the world, had shifted during the pandemic.

As the natural problem-solver that I am, I started thinking about new ideas. *What is it that our community is looking for right now?* It was as if I were going back to building my business from the beginning, back to the basics of how to nail our digital offer. I recalled every conversation I'd had with customers over the previous six months through our Facebook group, the support emails, and our live coaching calls. *What was it they were asking for without actually asking for it? What was it they wanted? What were their complaints? What were their dreams?*

The two concepts that were constantly popping up for our community were the desire to find more customers—especially since in-person contact had been halted due to the pandemic—and a desire to run their business more efficiently.

Even though the world had seemed to slow down, their to-do lists were longer than ever. Yet since a number of people had been living over the past year in fear that their health was going to be threatened—some even worrying that they might never see their extended family again—it drove people's desire for more time and freedom to build memories and experience life with loved ones.

Our customers needed a way to reach more people. They needed to grow their business faster. In fact, they needed to be able to do it in a way that allowed them to work half as much. The two words that popped into my head were "website" and "automation." Funny enough, I had been fighting the idea of teaching people how to build a website for the past year and a half, preferring to teach people how to create digital courses instead. But I realized that they couldn't scale their digital business the way they wanted if they didn't have an automated website and funnel.

It's funny how the universe will bring an idea you've pushed to the side back around if it's what you're meant to do. If you keep getting the nudge to do something, it could be a sign it's what you are supposed to do.

We revamped the existing business so we weren't losing money every month and built upon the already-developed digital-marketing and business-growth tools. Build a Blissful Business was born as a new offer to help our customers reach people online and sell faster working fewer hours.

Build a Blissful Business is robust, and the concept is simple. It provides all the strategy, templates, and tutorials that entrepreneurs need to:

1. Build a strong foundation for their business so that it will grow with them for decades and they won't get stuck after a year or two needing to start over.
2. Create a standout brand that people want to be a part of so they are constantly bringing in new customers.
3. Attract dream customers who make them love every ounce of what they do so the work doesn't feel like work.
4. Craft and sell their products or new digital offer on autopilot through high-converting funnels and a persuasive website while they sleep.

We launched the first version of Build a Blissful Business having no idea how it would go. I was hopeful we would change lives and turn the business around. Our very first launch, we had a hundred students who paid in full and several others who went with the payment plan, generating over $140,000 in revenue. We were back! The success of the launch felt amazing. I was hopeful for the first time in months that we had found our way.

It was in this year of business that I learned some of the most valuable lessons about building my business and assessing my success. Assessing your business regularly is important so you can pivot quickly when things aren't going well. It's no fun to look back and see that you had been losing money for the past six months when it could have been avoided.

Forty-five percent of small businesses fail within the first five years, and 65 percent fail within the first 10 years.[6] There are many different reasons why this happens, and the best way to determine whether your business will succeed is to keep a steady pulse on your finances. Regardless of all the little reasons *why* a business fails, it ultimately fails because it simply runs out of money.

As a visionary, numbers and data can feel hard because it might not be your area of expertise. It's difficult because when you have to get into data mode and crunch numbers, it takes you out of that fun visionary process. However, it is also an integral part of a successful business. Crunching numbers is like tending to a garden, where each calculation is a seed carefully planted or acknowledgement that a weed needs to be pulled. By nurturing and analyzing these numbers, you cultivate the fertile ground of your business, ensuring its growth and prosperity.

Though the numbers might not be as fun, they are important to track every single month so you don't find yourself where we were: at the highest of highs and then the lowest of lows. When I look deep down, I realize that I had avoided looking at the numbers because it was going to be too hard for me to see, not because I didn't know how to interpret them. The numbers were going to show me that some of the decisions I had made may not have been the best for my business. But as Melissa Houston says in her book *Cash Confident*, "The numbers will never lie to you. They may tell you what you don't want to hear, but don't be afraid or shy away from them because they offer you the most valuable information to help keep your business alive."[7]

Thankfully, I learned to tackle the numbers and adapt accordingly so we could continue serving in the way we loved and be able to continue our dream life. I can now give you the benefit of hindsight as you build your businesses.

Key Mistakes We Made that You Can Avoid

We tried to accommodate everyone.

We had been treating our inbox as a to-do list, operating from a state of wanting to accommodate the needs of every customer. If they asked for a resource, we created it, no matter how many hours it would take our team or the focus it would pull from other areas. What I learned is that you can't please everyone—and if you try to, you are actually doing both your business and your customers a disservice.

Remember: ultimately *you* are the one who knows your business best. Though your customers may ask for things, those things may not be in the best interest of the business. You are the expert, and it is your job to be able to navigate through all the requests to determine what is best for both the business and your customers' success. At the end of the day, if the business can't survive, then you won't be able to help anyone. Therefore, making decisions for the business is one of the best ways to serve your community.

I'm not saying you should never listen to what your customers and community are saying in your email support inbox. After all, your support email is one of the best places to get feedback and ideas for new things in your business. But it's all about how you look at it. Don't use it as your to-do list but rather as a tool to keep a pulse on how your business is operating, improve what you are doing, and get inspiration for new irresistible offers.

For example, if you are getting multiple similar questions from new customers, use this as a sign that you may want to take a deeper look at your onboarding process or content. If you are getting multiple requests for something, use it to determine whether this suggests a potential great new offer to launch to your community.

Lastly, recognize that when one or two people are emailing you with nasty comments, they don't represent *everyone*—and you don't need to change your entire business to please them. If you are a natural people pleaser, then you will want to be extra careful that you don't fall into the trap of assuming that one email complaint is a reflection of what everyone else is experiencing. Stay true to yourself, your values, your vision, your ideal customers, and the plan to keep focused. Don't let a few naysayers throw you off track and down a rabbit hole you can't come back from.

We didn't leverage A/B testing.
A/B testing is when you put something out with two different versions to see which works better. As a digital creator, your goal is to create content that resonates with your audience and drives engagement. A/B testing is like having a magic wand that allows you to experiment and optimize your creations to perfection.

Think of A/B testing as a scientific approach to creativity. It involves creating two versions of your content, A and B, with a slight variation between them. It could be a different headline, color scheme, or even call to action. You then expose these versions to your audience and measure their responses. Admittedly, we did this only a little and not as often as we could have—and the only time we did this well was when we were paying for ads. We would test an ad for the same offer but use different images, or we would use the same image but a different headline, or we would use the same headline but different caption or call to action.

There are many other places you can apply an A/B test to see how your audience responds and which approach is best. You can use it with email subject lines to determine which gets better open rates, or even content in your social posts. Create one post with the same five tips as an image and one as an Instagram Reel. See what performs best.

A/B testing is essential to help you:

1. Unveil audience preferences: A/B testing allows you to understand your audience's preferences and behavior. By comparing the performance of different versions, you can identify what resonates best with your audience, whether it's a specific design element, tone of voice, or content format.

2. Optimize engagement: Your ultimate goal as a digital creator is to captivate and engage your audience. A/B testing helps you fine-tune your content to maximize engagement. By testing different variations, you can identify the elements that generate higher click-through rates (meaning that people are clicking on your content), longer time spent on your content, and increased conversions.

3. Enhance conversion rates: Whether you're selling products, promoting services, or seeking subscriptions, conversions are vital. It's literally the difference between becoming successful and not. A/B testing enables you to optimize your conversion rates by experimenting with different strategies. You can test various layouts, pricing

models, or even the placement of your call-to-action buttons to find the winning combination that drives more conversions.

4. Offer continuous improvement: A/B testing is not a one-time activity but rather an ongoing process of improvement. As a digital creator, you need to adapt to changing trends, audience preferences, and market dynamics or your business won't survive past the five-year mark. A/B testing allows you to stay ahead by constantly experimenting, learning, and evolving your content strategy.

Remember: A/B testing is not about being right or wrong; it's about learning and refining your creative process. Embrace it as a powerful and fun tool that empowers you to create content that truly resonates with your audience, drives engagement, and ultimately leads to your success as a digital creator. This is a time when it's important to let your creativity flow and to not shy away from bizarre ideas. Test your off-the-wall concept against something a little more grounded and see what works.

We changed multiple things at once.

If you notice that things aren't "working" or are starting to go backward (your sales are down or people aren't engaging) and you need to make a shift, do it slowly. I'm not talking about waiting months between changes, but definitely don't do what we did and make several drastic moves all at once. Otherwise, you will never know what *actually* made or broke your business.

Every year on our business anniversary, we would do something *big,* such as launch a new feature, rebrand the website, or make improvements people had asked for. In 2020, we spared no expense to make it the biggest anniversary celebration our business had seen. We invested in a developer to help us add features to the website that would allow for better customer experience. With this change, we decided to restructure our offers, rebrand our website, change our sign-up process, and increase our prices. We literally changed everything we possibly could except for the content, all based on things we *thought* would help improve the customer experience and increase conversions. But boy, were we wrong! In the end, we had no idea what was causing the decline in memberships because we'd seemingly changed everything all at once.

Make a list of the things you think could be improved or might be causing a problem in your business and then pick one thing to change and test. Give it enough time for you to acquire data and then reassess. For example, if you have built an automated funnel and no one is joining your email list, then you need to determine whether it's a traffic issue, meaning you aren't sending enough people to it (see below). Lack of views tells me that people aren't visiting the page.

Views All Time	Opt-ins All Time	Conversion Rate All Time
8	0	0%

If you see a lot of traffic on the page but the percentage of people opting in is low, then it's likely that either the copy needs to be improved or you are sending the wrong audience to the page.

Views All Time	Opt-ins All Time	Conversion Rate All Time
5,154	1,118	22%

Look at the analytics of each section of your funnel, such as opt-in page, email open and click rates, and sales-page analytics, to analyze where you may need to make improvements. If you make an adjustment, give yourself enough time to collect new data to determine whether your changes were effective. Adjusting piece by piece will allow you to get a good gauge on what is affecting your business.

We didn't track analytics weekly, monthly, and quarterly.
Keeping a steady pulse on your business's finances will allow you to make decisions based on what the business needs. At the end of the day, if you don't keep a steady pulse on your numbers, then you may fall victim to the statistic of the 45 percent of businesses that fail in the first five years.[8] Following the numbers and assessing your analytics from day one can help prevent your business from getting too far past the point of no return.

Which analytics should you use?

In the financial department, you should be keeping track of your weekly expenses and comparing them to your weekly income. In his book *Traction,* Gino Whitman recommends checking them weekly to keep a pulse on your business that allows you to know exactly what's going on and be able to shift before things get too out of control.[9]

At the end of every month, pull your P&L. We do this via QuickBooks, but any simple bookkeeping software should be able to accomplish this for you. The P&L will show you the financial health of your business month to month, which you can compare quarter to quarter. It's important to know that some months will be more profitable than others, but having a weekly pulse on your business and then looking at the financials in a three-month time span can help you have a clear perspective on the numbers. It will allow you to see trends in your business and identify seasons that are more or less profitable to help you manage your business accordingly.

If you recognize that your sales trend up every summer, then maybe it's because your clientele is more likely to buy what you offer during that time of year. You can then shift your marketing efforts and spending to double or triple in the summer since summer is when your clients are buying the most. If you see a seasonal trend, ask yourself why and then lean into it to increase sales.

Your financials are like a tornado warning. Any consistent downturn is notifying you to look at your business and get serious about acting. However, instead of hiding in your basement under the covers when they get bad, use this as an opportunity to pull out your curiosity and detective skills to determine why and find the solution. Doing this will help you get ahead of any downturns before it's too late.

Lastly, remember that your financial mishaps do not define you. I will repeat this for those in the back: **Your financial mishaps do not define you! You are a badass no matter your mistakes because you are willing to take responsibility**. If you goofed, learn from your mistakes, adjust, and keep going.

We held onto contractors too long.
Hire slow and fire faster. I didn't realize the importance of this until we were breaking even with $30,000 in monthly revenue and $30,000 in contractor expenses. If I had been following the finances more closely and operating by this "hire slow and fire fast"

mentality, we would have never found ourselves in a breakeven state, nor would we have spent $6,000 a month for six months too long on a service that wasn't bringing in enough revenue to justify the cost.

Learn from your mistakes.

Looking back, I realize there were several times over the years that I kept contractors or software programs far longer than I should have. Firing contractors and employees remains one of the hardest responsibilities I have. No one likes to let people go, but as the CEO of your company, it's imperative that you don't wait too long to cut the cord. Otherwise, you may find yourself hemorrhaging cash with little return or wasting $36,000 that could have been making you money instead of wasting it.

I include software in the "fire fast" conversation because you need to constantly monitor it. If you are paying for analytics software but not using it, or maybe a software program you used for one launch but aren't currently using, it's wasted money to keep it on "staff." Cut it loose as quickly as possible. Though we keep a weekly pulse on the expenses, every couple months we look through the expenses we have listed in a spreadsheet to determine whether we are still using the programs. If we aren't, it gets cut or canceled.

Set a quarterly budget for your business and stick to it. There will always be operating and software expenses, so spend wisely based on what you need the most to move the needle forward.

Refer back to chapter 9 when it comes to hiring to help you get an idea of what might be the most effective expense to take on with the biggest ROI. If you really want a deep dive and to learn how to be the CFO of your business, read *Cash Confident* by Melissa Houston.[10]

Not Creating New Offers to Sell to Existing Customers

There are three ways to bring in revenue for your business:

1. Bring in new customers.
2. Sell additional offers to your existing customers.
3. Increase prices.

Every time a customer asked for something, we would create it. I already warned you about the danger of saying yes to everyone, and one of the biggest mistakes we made was adding these new resources to the membership at no additional cost. Though doing so added tremendous value to our membership subscription, it was at the expense of generating additional revenue. It also conditioned our customers to always expect to get new offers for free. At first, it seemed to work well, but years in, we found ourselves wanting to launch new offers yet were left with a community that expected everything to be handed to them on a silver platter at no additional cost.

Though it is incredibly important to serve your new customers well, your existing customers are your hottest leads. They have already purchased from you and statistically are more likely to buy your next offer than is a stranger finding you for the first time. Therefore, if you constantly give your existing customers everything new for free, you are doing them and your business a disservice. Be mindful of what you are offering and protect your future offers. If you have worked through developing the vision for your product suite—which is all the offers you plan to have in the future—don't promise your existing customers future offers for free. You will find that when you launch your next offer, some of your most loyal customers will be the most eager and excited to pay full price for your next offer.

By working to avoid all the mistakes we made in our business and doing things *right* from the get-go, you are sure to see tremendous results.

CHAPTER 11

QUALITIES FOR SUCCESS

As you gain success, you also need to evolve. There is no way around it. I would be lying if I said I were the same person I was when I started this journey in 2012. If I were, I wouldn't be here. You will look at the world differently and value your relationships and your time differently. If you don't, you will find yourself in the same place you are right now: wondering if success is possible for you and wishing you had more time to be with those and do the things you love.

Running a business will test you to the ends of the earth. You will have great days, and you will have hard days. I'm living proof though that at the end of the day, it is all worth it.

Deep down in my heart, I know that you are capable. We may not have met yet, but the sheer fact that you invested in this book tells me that you have that flame inside you—the flame that is needed to be a successful business owner. This book was intended to give that flame oxygen to grow until you are unstoppable. It also shows me that you are open and willing to learn new things, and this is exactly what you will need to be a successful entrepreneur.

The most successful entrepreneurs are constantly working on themselves, improving their mindsets to shift in ways that allow them to expand. If you are unable to evolve as a person, then your business won't be able to evolve. If your business doesn't evolve, then you will fall victim to the 45 percent that fail within the first five years.[11] I don't want that for you—and more importantly, do you want that for yourself?

You need to want your business to succeed more than anyone else does—more than your coach, more than your partner, more than your best friend. It is your responsibility to find the oxygen to fuel that flame inside you. And as that flame starts to grow and you begin to see success, you will need to evolve and expand to make room for a bigger fire.

If you want success, be willing to evolve and expand as both an individual and a business owner. Here are some key strategies I have found helpful to shift to the next level of business. Take them with you when you finish reading the book—remember them, use them, and watch the transformation!

Trust yourself.

You have a knowing light inside you. If it has dimmed—leaving you second-guessing your every move and unable to make decisions—then dig deep to understand why. What happened in your life to make you stop trusting yourself? Don't let this moment steal away your inner trust. You know yourself better than anyone else does, so trust your gut and move on. As you begin to trust yourself more, you can use your intuition, coupled with data, to make insightful decisions for your business.

Embrace your creative mind and let it wander.

It's oftentimes the craziest ideas that turn into the most magical outcomes. Though business can be challenging, it can also be playful and fun. Channel your inner child and creativity to come up with new ideas. I have always been inspired by Steve Jobs asking, "Why can't we have a thousand songs in our pocket?"[12] Through his curiosity, through his desire to dream, and by letting his creative mind flow, the iPod was born—and that little device changed our lives forever. Like Jobs, continue to create new offers and think of creative ways to promote them.

Be willing to try new things and look dumber than everyone else.

It's the brave explorers venturing into the unknown who find new lands. Growth doesn't happen inside your comfort zone, and it doesn't happen overnight. Many believe they need to get courage before they can try something new—recording your first YouTube video, holding your first workshop. In reality, courage is being afraid and doing it anyway. As you do it scared, again and again, you gain confidence, leading to an incredible shift and allowing you to go places in your business you'd never gone before.

Solicit feedback.

None of us is as smart as all of us. Though you may be very knowledgeable in certain areas, there is always room to learn from others who have gone before you. Be open to what they have to say and always ask, "Why?" Asking helps you understand at a deeper level, allowing you to think more critically. It's easy to find yourself sticking to what has worked in the past, but business is about innovation. Leverage what you learn from others to stay innovative in your business so you can keep up with both your customers and the latest trends.

Be curious.

Taking the time to research and teach yourself something new helps build confidence like you wouldn't believe! An important part of this as the CEO of your business is to *plan ahead and set regular goals.* Running a business without goals is like shopping for dinner groceries when you have no idea what you are going to make. At the end of the shopping trip, you have spent hundreds of dollars only to get home and still feel like you don't have the right ingredients to make a proper meal.

Instead of operating on a day-to-day plan to survive another week, come up with a revenue goal that you want to achieve in five years, then three years, and then one year. Then break down the next 12 months into quarters with just two to three goals for each quarter. We call these "big rocks," but you may also hear them referred to as "KPIs" or "key performance indicators." These are the key things you will focus on in the next quarter. A big rock could be launching your offer or a podcast, or it could be developing a more efficient system for your onboarding process. All four quarters will have a compounding effect, allowing you to reach your annual goal. Your annual goal should lead you to your three-year goal, and your three-year goal to your five-year goal.

Whenever you start to feel unfocused, bring yourself back to your goals. Are you focusing your energy and efforts on reaching your goals, or are you taking a detour that will take you off course? When most people find themselves faltering, they change their goals so their original ones don't seem so important and they can feel better about not having reached them fully. Don't be "most people." Learn to say what you mean, set goals you really want to achieve in the time frame you want to achieve them, and do what you said. If you fail, reassert your goal and take responsibility for making it happen. If you are someone with a wandering mind or who likes to take on a million projects at once, setting two to three goals per quarter will help keep you hyper-focused and from overextending yourself, thus making you more productive.

Keep expanding your network.

No business is built in a vacuum. Your network plays an invaluable role in your ability to reach more people with less effort. One of the quickest, most effective ways to network with people is to actually get in the same room with them. Nothing builds relationships faster than a face-to-face conversation.

Before the 2020 pandemic, I would jump at every opportunity to attend conferences or conventions. After the world started to meet back up in person, one of the first big conferences I attended was a Kajabi Hero Live event. This was a live conference for Kajabi users who were building their businesses online—many of which are my ideal customers. For a split second, I debated whether to attend. I only knew two other people going, and I wasn't sure if it was an investment in the business I wanted to make at that time. But something kept nudging me to make it work. I showed up to the event and connected with a friend of mine, who invited me out to dinner with six other powerful, badass women who had built million-dollar businesses and investment portfolios. We had great conversations in which I learned more about them and their businesses.

I found myself sitting directly next to Mya Nichol, a 23-year-old Instagram sensation with hundreds of thousands of followers and who had built a $1 million business in under two years. I was able to hear about her journey, which led to more personal topics and an instant connection after we learned that we both love wake surfing. Over the course of the three-day event, I found myself sitting next to her multiple times, having more and more conversations. By the end of the convention, we had a solid plan to bring her on our podcast and have her teach a workshop for my community and contribute to a revenue-generating opportunity. It is highly unlikely that a connection like this would have been made via Instagram, especially since her DM inbox is always full, and it would have been much harder for me to stand out among the rest.

Put in the effort to get in the room with people who are more successful than you and have tried harder things than you and then learn from them. Attend the annual conference, engage inside virtual communities, and participate in local networking events. Genuinely build relationships with others and approach them with a "give more than you take" mentality. If you are open and give to others, they will be more willing to give back. When your relationship grows, collaboration can take place. Instead of competing, you work together to both make a bigger impact.

Through years of networking and showing up for other coaches, offering training for their community, and giving feedback on their business, I have created a network of individuals who trust me and want to help me in return.

When you need rest, take it.

Building a business requires major energy. *You can't be on all the time.* You have a busy life with many more responsibilities than in your business. Though you are someone who isn't afraid to get your hands dirty and work hard, it's important to rest when you need it. Take a workday off without feeling guilty. Binge watch an entire season of *Love Is Blind* and don't feel bad about it. You deserve to take time off to re-energize—in fact, you *need* it. You can't grow and scale a million-dollar business if you are too burned out to get out of bed!

Shift with the seasons of life.

No matter what you do, life around you will constantly be moving, shifting, and evolving. As much as you wish you could, you can't control it. You will without a doubt experience different seasons when things move fast and then slow. Your seasons could shift as frequently as the daily tides or last as long as the Earth takes to circle the Sun.

The one constant to remember is that whatever the season, it won't last forever. You are strong, you are capable, and you can problem-solve your way around any difficult situation. I know this because you have made it to the end of this book. And I don't care if it took you months to get here. All I care about is that, after taking time away, you came back to this because you want more. You want more for yourself, you want more for your family, and you want more for your clients.

No matter what season you are in, click the "easy" button whenever you can. Buy the template, set up the automation, use AI, and hire a coach to walk you through the necessary steps.

These easy buttons aren't a cop-out. They are the ticket to more vacations to the tropics without opening your computer and more face-to-face time with your favorite people. They are the secret to thousands of dollars rolling into your bank account while you are sleeping and living your very best life. Dream on . . . and then take action!

ONE LAST THING

I am incredibly grateful that you bought this book and made it to the end—or skipped to the end (no judgment!). Your dedication to your business and willingness to seek help by getting this book tells me you will go far. I see incredible accomplishments in your future, and I want to celebrate you for taking this simple first step in your business.

To celebrate, **take a picture of this book** in your favorite reading spot (unless it's on the toilet), **share the picture to your stories and tag me @thekrissychin_**! I can't wait to shout you out and celebrate you on my IG.

I have one more small ask, if you aren't against it. If you found value in this book, head over to Amazon and leave an honest review. It won't cost you a penny, it will take less than 60 seconds, and I will be forever grateful.

PRO TIP

If you want to earn 1,000 brownie points from your mentors, leave reviews on their books and podcasts! It is one of the easiest and cheapest ways to show your gratitude, and they will love the heck out of you for it.

Keep learning for free!

Instagram: Follow me on Instagram @TheKrissyChin_ for quick tips to automate and grow your business.

Podcast: If you like listening, I have a podcast called *Badass Is the New Black* where you can tune in to short episodes and interviews to improve your mindset, marketing, and business skills. Kandc-creative.com/podcast

Youtube: We have a growing YouTube channel where Claire and I share step-by-step tutorials as well as podcast episodes. Scan this QR code to subscribe now!

NEXT STEPS TO BUILD
YOUR BLISSFUL BUSINESS

Ready to take everything you learned here, create your offer, and build your website and automated funnels to sell while you sleep?

Explore Build a Blissful Business at kandccreative.com/book-bbb.
Build a Blissful Business is a step-by-step program with access to our
in-depth training, tech tutorials, pre-built copywriting, design, and
Canva templates to get your business online in half the time.

Workbook

Training Center

Branding + Templates

Comprehensive Lessons + Tech Tutorials

By the end of Build a Blissful Business, you will have:

- a millionaire's mindset
- an irresistible offer that sells itself
- clarity on your ideal customer
- a beautifully designed website that draws in dream customers
- and an automated funnel to sell while you sleep

Scan to learn more ⟶

ACKNOWLEDGMENTS

This book is by far the hardest educational resource I have created and a journey that took three years from the first outline to publish day. Though part of me is still in shock that I made it here, the other part of me isn't surprised at all because I know how great of a support system I have. It really is this group of people that made this all possible.

I want to first acknowledge and thank my husband Michael for always being in my corner and one of my biggest supporters. I met Michael a few months after I started my very first business as a nutrition response testing (NRT) practitioner, and though I wasn't sure he truly believed in the "woo" I was doing through muscle testing, he showed up faithfully for his appointments and bought the supplements he tested for. He truly has been supporting my entrepreneurial journey since day one, and it means the world to me. I have been inspired watching him grow in our business ventures, and though it may not always seem like I appreciate his business advice and wisdom, I do. Michael has a special way of encouraging me to grow and be better while still loving me even when I don't apply his advice. There have been many moments where I needed unconditional support during this process, like when I hurt my back and needed him to step up in so many ways and he was there without complaints. He has been there to celebrate the highest of highs and has been able to calm me during the lowest of lows and assure me it will all be OK. I know it's not easy when I am working on a million projects at once, but he always shows up when I need him, and I couldn't ask for a better life partner.

Aside from the amazing book cover she designed, this book wouldn't be possible without my dear sister and business partner Claire VanBemmelen. She has stood alongside me from the very first phone call I made to convince her to bring GROworkspace to life without a guarantee she would ever get paid. I thank her for saying yes anyway. Her design skills and talents are the best I have ever seen, and I feel incredibly lucky to have her by my side, not only helping our business shine bright but, more importantly, helping our clients stand out online from everyone else. She has been such an incredible partner, never afraid to push back on my ideas (maybe that's the sister bond) and offer a fresh perspective. I wouldn't be here with a book to tell our story without her. The last seven years have been incredible, and I am even more excited for the years to come as I know we are just getting started and have so much more to give to this world.

I've already dedicated this book to my father, Robert VanBemmelen, but I want to acknowledge him here and show my gratitude for his heart and passion. He is the kind of person that no matter how bizarre he sounded or came off, he would share his inventions, passions, and conviction with you. He wanted the best for everyone and lived with knowledge and wisdom that often made him feel like an outcast. His passion and dedication to projects inspired me to take my ideas, put in the work, and bring them to life, including this book. I thank him for being him and never wavering or hiding for fear of rejection. He has touched the lives of more than one can imagine, and through this book, I continue to live out his legacy of making an impact on this world in my own unique way.

Thank you to my mom, Sandy VanBemmelen, and sister Carrie O'Connell for being on our support team over the years. Behind every business owner is an incredible support team, and we could not have done it without them both.

I also want to acknowledge my sister Katie Giordano for her bravery to go first. She invited me to do the NRT training with her that sparked my first business venture. She later invited me into the direct-sales venture she was pursuing, which was the catalyst for GROworkspace and helped me learn many lessons I shared in this book. Her gentle and loving support has always inspired me to grow as a friend, mother, and businesswoman.

I would love to acknowledge and thank Nicole Switala for being such an incredible support to Claire and me as our right-hand woman and integrator helping us execute and reach our goals and being willing to step in wherever needed to get the job done—and done well. It's her support in the business that allowed for more time and attention to writing this book. Her dedication hasn't gone unnoticed, and we feel lucky to have her here.

Thank you to Amelia Forczak and the entire Pithy Wordsmithery team for guiding me in this process of writing a book from the beginning outline all the way through self-publishing. Without them, this book would be just a bunch of scattered thoughts.

Amelia's team was incredible to work with, and I can tell they really cared about making this book worth reading.

Thank you to my mother-in-law, Elaine, for sitting by me at the dining-room table for weeks helping me rearrange the book when I realized I needed to rewrite it. Her willingness to help kept me from bailing on the project altogether.

Thank you to everyone who was mentioned in this book. Your willingness to share your stories and wisdom helped make this book what it is, and I know it will touch the lives of many for years to come.

Thank you to John Roussot and Ciara Rubin for being my writing accountability partners. Watching them both write their books kept me inspired to keep going and push through any hard days of feeling like the end would never come. I am so grateful for every text Ciara responded to as I was fleshing out the book, especially the title. Who knew titling a book could be so hard?! I appreciate their support in helping me lean into my intuition to make hard decisions during this process.

I want to share my immense gratitude for every student we have had over the years. I have learned so many invaluable lessons through helping them that I was able to include in this book. Their willingness to trust me and Claire and guide them in their entrepreneurial journey means the world to me, and I don't take it for granted.

ABOUT THE AUTHOR

Krissy Chin is a business coach and the host of the *Badass Is the New Black* podcast, where each week she teaches people how to start, grow, and automate their business online leveraging the things they are passionate about so they can create a life they don't have to take a vacation from. Though Krissy has dabbled in entrepreneurship since 2012, she found her first success in direct sales in 2014, allowing her to eventually leave her nursing job for good. With her instinct to problem-solve and work as efficiently as possible, she launched her own business, GROworkspace, in 2017 with her sister Claire VanBemmelen, providing business training and marketing materials for Young Living Brand Partners. GRO-workspace grew its paid membership to over 6,000 members in under a year and went from $0 to $1 million in revenue in under 20 months while only working part-time.

In 2019, she launched her podcast and website as a new resource to help others who want to take their knowledge and skills and turn them into a profitable online business working only part-time hours. Krissy brought Claire into this business in 2022 and rebranded as K and C Creative. Together, they are the most influential sister duo out there teaching aspiring entrepreneurs how to grow and scale their online businesses through high-converting websites and automated funnels.

She lives in Georgia, with her husband Michael, two kids, and Portuguese water dog Miss Tess.

RESOURCES

In addition to the downloadable workbook we created for you, we have put together a list of additional resources that coincide with the book (see below). For the most up-to-date list of resources with clickable links, scan this QR code.

Chapter 1

- *Badass is the New Black* Podcast Season 3, Episode 38, "Common Mistakes that Slow Down Your Success with Brad Bizjack."

- *Badass is the New Black* Podcast Season 4, Episode 2, "The GPS Framework to Accelerate Your Success."

Chapter 2

- Turn Your Knowledge into Passive Income extended exercise and PDF guide.

- How to create a course in seconds using AI—YouTube video.

- If you are interested in affiliate marketing and have a business audience, consider our program, Build a Blissful Business, as a product to promote. Our affiliates generate income in exchange for helping us market and sell our offers. You can earn a commission from every Build a Blissful Business sale you make. To inquire about our affiliate program, email support@kandccreative.com.

Chapter 3

- Free access to the Nail Your Digital Offer Workshop to help you pick the best digital offer for you and teach you how to make it irresistible.

Chapter 6

- I created a podcast, blog, and YouTube video where I break down my method for taking one piece of content and turning it into more than 10 pieces of both short- and long-form content. *Badass Is the New Black,* Season 4, Episode 4: "How to Repurpose Your Content to Reach More People."

Chapter 7

- Build a Blissful Business Program. Inside this program, we break down everything discussed in this chapter further with training, tech-tutorial videos, templates, and other resources that you will need to set up your brand, develop your offer, build your website, and create both your freebie and your funnel.

Platforms We Recommend for Website and Course Hosting

- Kajabi: the all-in-one platform we use to host our website, courses, and CRM system. Scan the QR code and use our referral link to get a free 30-day trial and our complementary Nail Your Digital Offer workshop. This workshop not only helps you identify your offer but also shows you how to position your offer as irresistible. We also include tech tutorials to help you create your first offer in Kajabi.

- AttractWell: an all-in-one platform we are very familiar with that creates templates and tutorials to teach others how to use the platform. Scan the QR code to use our referral link and get your first month for $1, your second month ½ off the regular price, plus an additional class and landing page.

- GetOiling: an all-in-one platform we are very familiar with that creates templates and tutorials to teach others how to use the platform. Owned by the creators of AttractWell, this platform is specifically for Young Living Brand Partners. Scan the QR code to use our referral link and get your first month for $1, your second month ½ off the regular price, plus an additional class and landing page.

- A comprehensive list of platforms and software that we recommend to run your business can be found at our website: kandccreative.com/tools.

Chapter 8

- Explore our ever-growing template shop with copy, designed landing pages, and Canva templates.

- The Scalable Podcast System: Interested in starting a podcast or already have one and want to look like a true professional with every automation integrated and the resources to set your guest up for success? Grab our scalable podcast system and all the templates. It is not only effective for solo podcasting but also highly valuable for podcasts that are bringing on guest speakers and need to manage back-and-forth communication.

- Step-by-step tutorial on how to set up Manychat to automatically respond to your Instagram comments.

- For step-by-step tech videos for various AI platforms, visit our YouTube channel.

Chapter 9

- Looking to hire a copywriter, graphic or website designer, or someone to help you set up your tech and automations? Hire our team for support! To get a custom quote for your project, access our Done-for-You services page and book a call.

- Access the Contract Club for incredibly affordable legal templates created by business and tax attorney Braden Drake.

Chapter 10

- Weekly tracker to keep track of important analytics for your business.

- If the multiple steps in your funnel are not performing well, consider the Profitable List-Building Blueprint course to help you rebuild your funnel with a better strategy.

ENDNOTES

1   Brenda Winkle, "Your Yes Filled Life," Brenda Winkle website, https://www.brendawinkle.com/about.

2   Knowledge Base, "Average industry rates for email as of September 2023," Constant Contact website, October 3, 2023, https://knowledgebase.constantcontact.com/email-digital-marketing/articles/KnowledgeBase/5409-average-industry-rates?lang=en_US.

3   John Turner, "How to Improve Your Email Marketing ROI (4 Tips)," *Forbes*, November 8, 2022, https://www.forbes.com/sites/theyec/2022/11/08/how-to-improve-your-email-marketing-roi-4-tips/?sh=45d19b0a60b3.

4   Kendra Cherry, "How to Achieve a State of Flow," Verywell Mind, March 28, 2023, https://www.verywellmind.com/what-is-flow-2794768#:~:text=It%20takes%20approximately%2010%20to,day%2C%20given%20the%20right%20conditions.

5   "The Life-Changing Magic of Tidying Up Quotes," Goodreads, https://www.goodreads.com/work/quotes/41711738-jinsei-ga-tokimeku-katazuke-no-maho#:~:text=The%20best%20way%20to%20choose,yardstick%20by%20which%20to%20judge.

6   Michael T. Deane, "Top 6 Reasons New Businesses Fail," Investopedia, December 30, 2022, https://www.investopedia.com/financial-edge/1010/top-6-reasons-new-businesses-fail.aspx#:~:text=Data%20from%20the%20BLS%20shows,to%2015%20years%20or%20more.

7   Melissa Houston, "Cash Confident: An Entrepreneur's Guide to Creating a Profitable Business," Melissa Houston CPA blog, https://melissahoustoncpa.com/cash-confident-book/.

8   Deane, "Top 6 Reasons New Businesses Fail."

9   EOS, "A Grip on Your Business," EOS website, https://www.eosworldwide.com/traction-book?utm_term=&utm_medium=ppc&utm_campaign=Dynamic+Brand&utm_source=adwords&hsa_net=adwords&hsa_ad=652314645782&hsa_mt=&hsa_acc=3066578213&hsa_src=g&hsa_tgt=dsa-83191683436&hsa_grp=151035902767&hsa_cam=19879578382&hsa_kw=&hsa_ver=3&gclid=Cj0KCQiAuqKqBhDxARIsAFZELmJD7Y9ilSmcuWmndbTs3laUq_OUZws_xxX7D-lO50ltCcv56znxGTLkaAsfYEALw_wcB.

10 Houston, "Cash Confident: An Entrepreneur's Guide to Creating a Profitable Business."

11 Deane, "Top 6 Reasons New Businesses Fail."

12 "Apple Music Event 2001-The First Ever iPod Introduction," YouTube, posted April 3, 2006, https://www.youtube.com/watch?v=kN0SVBCJqLs.

Made in the USA
Columbia, SC
26 September 2024

42466854R00115